PUBLISHING
Your Own
SPECIALIST MAGAZINE

PUBLISHING *Your Own* SPECIALIST MAGAZINE

Alan Greene

KOGAN PAGE

Copyright © Alan Greene 1990

All rights reserved. No reproduction, copy or transmission
of this publication may be made without written permission.

No paragraph of this publication may be reproduced, copied
or transmitted save with written permission or in accordance
with the provisions of the Copyright Act 1956 (as amended),
or under the terms of any licence permitting limited copying
issued by the Copyright Licensing Agency, 33-34 Alfred Place,
London WC1E 7DP.

Any person who does any unauthorised act in relation to
this publication may be liable to criminal prosecution and
civil claims for damages.

First published in Great Britain in 1990 by
Kogan Page Limited, 120 Pentonville Road,
London N1 9JN.

British Library Cataloguing in Publication Data
A CIP record for this book is available
from the British Library.

ISBN 0-85091-979-8

Typeset by DP Photosetting, Aylesbury, Bucks
Printed and bound in Great Britain by
Biddles Ltd, Guildford

Contents

Introduction	**3**
Which Magazine?	**5**
1. Financial Planning	**9**
Profit and loss/cash flow 11; Banks and accountants 16; Credit control 18	
2. Marketing and PR	**20**
The four Ps 20; Direct mail 22; Press advertising 26; Point-of-sale material 26; Public relations 27	
3. The Role of the Editor	**30**
Content and quality 30; Editing skills 31; Format and approach 31; Dealing with contributors 34; House style 34; Editing copy 38; Schedules 38; Page plans and proofs 38; Good PR 40	
4. Design	**41**
How do I find a designer? 41; Interviewing and briefing your designer 42; Designing the cover 43; Text pages 46	
5. Production	**47**
Printing 47; Paper 49; Typesetting 50; Origination 53; Finishing and binding 56; Choosing a printer 56	
6. Advertising	**61**
Advertising rates 61; Who will sell your space? 65; Advertising production 67	
7. Distribution	**69**
Subscription sales 69; Newsagent sales 73; Other distribution 76	
Glossary	**78**
Useful Addresses	**85**
Further Reading	**95**
Index	**97**

Masculine pronouns have been used throughout this book. This stems from a desire to avoid ugly and cumbersome language, and no discrimination, prejudice or bias is intended.

Introduction

There has been a considerable increase in the number of magazine titles in the UK in recent years. General consumer publishing, particularly in the field of women's magazines, has seen some outstanding new title successes against competition from long-established magazines. Perhaps less spectacular but just as noticeable is the steady growth in specialist publishing. A considerable number of new magazines, often dealing with a specific or 'new angle' aspect of a subject, have sprung up in areas that have hitherto been covered by a few well-established magazines. Other established magazines which have been market leaders are finding their position challenged by newer titles which take a fresh approach.

These newer titles are often brought out by small publishers keen to find and fill market needs unnoticed or ignored by the larger firms. This trend, together with the impact of the computer and new technology generally, has revolutionised the physical process of printing and made it easier for the individual or small company to publish a magazine.

The purpose of this book is to explain, in a non-technical way, the process of publishing a magazine, from the initial idea through to the final stage, when the magazine reaches the hands of the reader. Although it includes essential information for the publisher who is doing it for profit, it should also be of interest and practical use to those engaged in producing house magazines, and small non profit-making publications, as well as students of the trade.

The book covers all the functions and jobs needed to produce a magazine each of which, in a large publishing company, would often be the work of a whole department. It is impossible to cover all the topics in great detail and readers who wish to find out more about a particular aspect should turn to some of the many books available.

As the publisher of a specialist magazine for some years, I have learned many of the things covered in this book the hard way. I hope that some of the advice given here will be of practical use to those new to publishing.

Alan Greene

Which Magazine?

A recent survey has highlighted the growth of magazines in this country. Over the past ten years the number of general interest magazines has risen by nearly 70 per cent to 2289 and business interest titles by nearly 65 per cent to 4263. In this period there has been a 40 per cent growth in copy sales and the share of advertising from the total spend in the UK is increasing. This is good news for magazine publishers because it indicates that the market for magazines is growing. The interesting thing is that there are no safe bets in the race; if there were then the large publishing conglomerates would clean up. It is not just a matter of identifying a new fashion or trend and throwing money and big company resources at it. Thankfully, there is still room for the small-scale entrepreneur or the enthusiast. Magazines can establish a continuing contact with their readership which engenders loyalty and a unique relationship.

Magazines come and go, of course, and among the many which flower briefly and then die are hundreds of specialist magazines, some produced by large companies and others by small independent companies or individuals. Statistics show that, of the new magazines of this kind started each year, only 15 per cent or so will make it to the end of their first year and of those, the majority will take over three years to get into real profit. Many of these failures have been caused by lack of planning, and ignorance of the fairly complex business of publishing a magazine *and* keeping it going.

The wish to publish a magazine may come from a personal interest in the subject, combined with the essential desire to make money somewhere along the line. Although the would-be publisher with a specialist interest or knowledge can make it work, the need for financial planning as explained in Chapter 1 is essential. It is only too easy to underestimate the amount of money needed to fund a publication and ventures which are under-financed have a very slim chance of making it. Even vaguely planned publications which are costed to start making a profit from the first issue, which is then supposed to pay for the second issue, are not unknown. There never is a second issue.

6   **Publishing Your Own Specialist Magazine**

Should you look for the much talked about 'gap in the market'? Yes, but be careful; very often gaps exist for a very good reason. Until recently general magazines for men, along the lines of women's magazines, with features on clothes, travel, style and so on, just did not exist. It was a gap that no one was prepared to fill until recently when a couple of seemingly successful titles have appeared.

On the other hand, one look at the titles that exist at the moment shows that there is room for the most abstruse subjects. There seem to be very few subject areas which do not have a magazine covering them. Who would have thought that there would be a magazine on ham radio, or early church music, or carriage driving or map collecting, even a magazine on amusement arcade machines? Is there room for more than two magazines on amusement arcade machines? An instant gut-feeling says no, but there are no less than three magazines on coin collecting, four on country and western music and six on stamp collecting.

What about a magazine in an area where there seem to be too many already? Well, a large number of titles means a very active market area and it may be easier to carve a sliver off a large market than a chunk off a small one. There are, for example, 12 magazines on golf, 62 on various aspects of computing, and 89 on religion of various kinds. Motoring has 106 but among these are small, niche market publications on, for example, veteran cars, *deux cheveaux*, and restoring classic cars, which appeal to a distinct area of the market. There is room in a crowded market with the big boys, you just have to know exactly which part of it you are going for.

Many smaller, and indeed some larger, magazines have as their base readership members of a club or society. Although this is no guarantee of success it does help to underpin a circulation base.

If the magazine you are contemplating comes from a personal interest because you feel there is a particular need for something that does not exist, or something that you believe could be done better and more successfully, do as much research as you can. You may envisage a better produced, more upmarket version of a magazine that already exists. Consider the market and the readers carefully. Will they pay more for better pictures? Are they buying the magazine simply for the diary listing or some other feature which means that a cheap and cheerful magazine is all they want? How can you best attract advertisers away from an existing magazine to your new untested one? You may find that you will want to alter your editorial approach substantially in the light of what you discover.

Think too about your own skills and aspirations when you consider the project. In a large publishing company you will have a number of executives carrying out specific jobs: Sales Manager, Production Manager, Editor, Circulation and Subscription Manager and Financial Manager as well as the Publisher who endeavours to keep the whole thing together. With a small magazine you will have to combine some of these functions and it would be as well to decide on your own abilities as well as those who are working with you.

Is there room in the already crowded market for a new publication? The answer is unquestionably yes. Among all the failures, many newcomers make it. But they only make it with hard work, dedication, luck and most importantly - planning.

Chapter 1
Financial Planning

Financial planning is essential in any enterprise, large or small. Even if you are running a parish magazine or a subsidised house journal, it is important to be able to predict, as accurately as possible, your costs and revenue and form a budgeting strategy.

If you plan to make your magazine into a business which will grow and make profits, almost the first thing you must do is to sit down and draw up a financial forecast. You will need it to plan your way ahead, and as we shall see later in this chapter, if you need to raise money to finance the venture, a well-thought out business plan is essential. It is also the only way to concentrate your mind on every aspect of producing and selling your magazine.

When you begin to consider the details of your magazine by working on the forecast you will find that problems arise for which you can find solutions in advance, problems that could prove to be difficult or impossible to solve if you confronted them when the magazine was up and running. Although the figures and calculations are important, you are also forced to consider the way your business will actually work, and the necessity of putting figures in boxes does not allow you to gloss over difficult questions.

Do not be tempted to start publishing without tackling this very important, though admittedly tedious, exercise. Access to a computer and spread-sheet software like Supercalc or Lotus 123 will save a great deal of time, although a blank sheet of paper, a ruler and pencil will do as well even though in the long run it is more time-consuming and a lot less flexible.

Figure 1.1 is a simple example of a first-year profit and loss exercise for a magazine publishing enterprise. It must be stressed that the figures shown here merely illustrate the points made below and are in no way intended to be an accurate reflection of the figures you are likely to come across when costing your own magazine.

Specialist Magazine X	Nov	Dec	Jan	Feb	Mar	Apr	May	Jun	Jul	Aug	Sep	Oct	Total
Units													
Subscriptions		800	900	100	1100	1200	1300	1300	1400	1400	1400	1500	12400
Newsagent sales		15000	12000	12000	12000	12000	12000	12000	12000	12000	12000	12000	135000
Specialist trade sales		1000	1000	1000	1000	1000	1000	1000	1000	1000	1000	1000	11000
Overseas trade sales		4500	4500	4500	4500	4500	4500	4500	4500	4500	4500	4500	49500
Total		21300	18400	17600	18600	18700	18800	18800	18900	18900	18900	19000	207900
Revenue													
Subscriptions (cover price 2.25													
sub price 20.00)		2667	3000	333	3667	4000	4333	4333	4667	4667	4667	5000	41333
Newsagent distribution		16031	12825	12825	12825	12825	12825	12825	12825	12825	12825	12825	144281
Specialist trade sales		900	1013	113	1238	1350	1463	1463	1575	1575	1575	1688	13950
Overseas trade sales		4050	4050	4050	4050	4050	4050	4050	4050	4050	4050	4050	44550
Advertising		8000	4000	4000	5000	6000	6000	6000	6000	6000	6000	6000	63000
Total		31648	24888	21821	26779	28225	28671	28671	29117	29117	29117	29563	307115
Direct Costs													
Design and artwork		1900	1900	1900	1900	1900	1900	1900	1900	1900	1900	1900	20900
Print and paper		16000	14000	14000	14000	14000	14000	14000	14000	14000	14000	14000	15600
Typesetting		1000	1000	1000	1000	1000	1000	1000	1000	1000	1000	1000	11000
Editorial		3000	3000	3000	3000	3000	3000	3000	3000	3000	3000	3000	33000
Subscription mailings		1200	1200	1200	1200	1200	1200	1200	1200	1200	1200	1200	13200
Advertising costs		1500	1000	1000	1000	1000	1000	1000	1000	1000	1000	1000	11500
Promotion		8000	3000								5000			
TOTAL		32600	25100	22100	22100	22100	22100	22100	22100	27100	22100	22100	245600
Profit/Loss		−952	−213	−779	4679	6125	6571	6571	7017	2017	7017	7463	45515

Figure 1.1. *Example of a first-year profit and loss sheet*

Profit and loss/cash flow

There are two ways you will need to look at your financial projections: one is as *profit and loss* per issue and per year, and the other is as *cash flow* over the year. Both are important but, simply put, profit and loss shows your profitability, and cash flow shows whether you can maintain sufficient funds to produce the profit over a period.

As you will see, Figure 1.1 is not concerned with overheads, such as office rent, heat, light, telephones and so on, merely the direct income and outgoings of the publication itself. Let us look at the various headings which are spread over the months of the year.

Units

How many copies of the magazine are you going to sell each month and how are you going to sell them? You may be involved in a publication which is given away to a defined readership in order to provide an audience for advertisers. This kind of publication is known as 'controlled circulation' and would, of course, require a far higher advertising revenue.

Subscriptions

If you are going to offer your magazine on subscription, usually an important element of a specialist magazine's finances, you must make some assumptions about the number of new subscriptions that you will receive at any time. This could happen in several different ways.

If you promote subscriptions in advance of your first issue by mailing groups and societies and perhaps putting leaflets in competitive magazines, you should get a 'bulge' of subscriptions to begin with, followed by a regular flow as you promote subscriptions within the magazine. You may decide to promote subscriptions after two or three issues have been published, in which case the bulge would come later. From a profit and loss point of view it would be most practical to establish how many subscriptions you are likely to get in a year and use this as a monthly average figure (as shown in Figure 1.1). You will, of course, be sending out to your complete subscription list every month, assuming that this is the frequency of the magazine.

You may want to send out free copies of your magazine to influential people or it may be that yours is a controlled-circulation magazine which relies on free distribution to attract advertisers. Remember that there is a cost attached to this and unless the quantity is very small you might want to show the numbers which are given away free in a separate line from the paid subscribers.

Depending on the nature of your magazine you may also need to have a separate line for overseas subscriptions. If these are likely to be significant then the units will need to be shown separately as the income will be different from UK subscriptions because of the higher rates charged.

Newsagent sales

This area is likely to form the biggest category of any commercial magazine and is a notoriously difficult one to plan for at the outset. You should take advice from your chosen distributor and find out the newsagent circulation of your competitors' magazines. This can be found in *British Rate and Data* or from the magazines themselves by pretending to be a (carefully disguised) 'advertiser' looking for a potential advertising medium. What usually happens, bearing in mind that these copies are on sale or return, is that your distributor recommends that you supply more than the 'guesstimate' or the base circulation figure you need to aim at.

For a general title with wide potential consumer appeal this could mean many more copies indeed, and the economics of being paid for, say, half the number of copies you print needs to be examined very carefully. However, with a specialist magazine the chances are that this risk can be minimised, although your initial supply for the newsagents will have to be high to make an impact and obtain sufficient coverage. Your figures here will need to reflect this initial high wastage of copies although this should settle down after the first few issues.

Specialist trade sales

This may or may not apply to your proposed magazine, but it is common to many magazines that there is an area of sale to trade, ie 'non-individual' customers, not covered by your main newsagent distributor. For example, in the case of a cycling magazine, cycle shops, or a boating magazine, yacht chandlers or clubs; in fact, anyone you supply on a regular basis with magazines at a discount. Again, you may wish to pre-mail these potential outlets with a brochure inviting them to order or send them the first issue to show them your product.

As far as planning goes you will most likely be guessing at numbers but perhaps not entirely in the dark. It is probably best to look at the market 'universe' (how many cycle shops are there in the country?) and take a considered view of the possible percentage likely to respond. Be realistic and err on the side of caution. Also remember that, however wonderful your magazine is, people in the business will take a while to become aware of it. Your month by month unit sale figure may need to take account of a gentle growth in numbers sold to this sector.

Overseas trade sales
These depend very much on whether your magazine will 'travel' in terms of subject matter. Sales will usually be slow to start and then settle down to a regular pattern.

Revenue
The income or revenue can now be calculated line by line according to the units in the section above.

Subscriptions
Your revenue each month, averaging the subscriptions income, will be the annual figure multiplied by the annual subscription fee divided by 12 for each month of the year.

Newsagent distribution
The sum here depends on the discount you have negotiated with the distributor. This varies, but you will probably be giving 50 per cent or more - 52.5 per cent to the distributor is common. So, as you see, the sum here is the quantity sold less discount.

Specialist trade sales
The same applies here, except that the discount given away will be less as you will probably be dealing direct with retailers rather than wholesalers, so 25-30 per cent discount is more likely. We have used an average of 27.5 per cent.

Overseas trade sales
Discounts of 50-60 per cent will usually apply, although if you deal with overseas distributors yourself rather than going through a middleman, on a sale or return basis, you get away with 40 per cent discount. We have used 60 per cent discount in the example.

Advertising
Your advertising revenue will need to be put in here. Your income will depend very much on the targets you have set and it will be clear that if you are running a commercial publication this is a

14   **Publishing Your Own Specialist Magazine**

very important, if not crucial, figure. Remember that you may anticipate your magazine taking, say, 12 pages of advertising but they will be composed of a variety of different sizes of space, selling at different prices.

Costs

This is the section where the sober realities of the cost of producing a magazine come into play. How precisely you want to break this section up is entirely up to you and for simplicity's sake you may want, for example, to put all print and production costs under one heading. It is quite useful, however, to break down your costs as much as you can so that if (as you should) you use this layout as a budgeting tool, you can see the relative costs of various activities at a glance and trace variations of cost.

Production costs

From the quotations supplied by printers, typesetters and so on you will have a fairly accurate idea of your production costs, and you can begin to allocate them to each month or issue. (See Chapter 5 for an explanation of the terms used.)

Be aware of the fixed costs - origination, design, typesetting - as opposed to the variable costs of paper and printing. It is wise to allow a margin of error on the fixed costs to allow room for your errors and changes of mind. The print and paper price from your printer should be exact as long as there have been no extra increases in paper prices since his quotation.

Editorial contributions

Although your individual payments to each contributor may vary you should set a budget within which the words and the pictures for the magazine are produced. It is likely that this will be a set figure which will not change much from issue to issue.

Subscription mailings

The cost of mailing your subscribers should remain fairly constant. Postage, enveloping and stuffing costs should be known factors.

Advertising commission

Commission paid to a freelance agent or company employed to obtain advertising for you at X per cent is a known factor which is directly related to your advertising income.

Financial Planning 15

Promotion costs
Mailings, advertising, PR – all these have to be carefully costed and set against the first issue or perhaps in a six-month preparatory profit and loss (P and L) plan, which will be more L than P in the pre-publication months.

With your columns for revenue and costs totalled up it is a simple matter to take one away from the other and see what kind of profits or losses you will be making.

Cash flow
Predicting cash flow is vital. It is easy to have a profitable magazine on paper which goes bust for lack of cash. Once you have fixed your revenue and cost figures per issue you should be able to work on the cash flow. The idea here is to place income and revenue in the months in which they occur, and this is easier to predict in some cases than others.

You will have negotiated terms of credit with your suppliers, for example. Although the usual terms of business are 30 days' credit it may be possible to negotiate more extended credit with some suppliers. Your printer, for example, might be prepared to give you 60 days or more credit if he sees the prospect of good regular work in the future. It is always worth a try. The commission you pay to the advertising space salesman or woman is likely to be paid on publication of the magazine as are payments to editorial contributors, although some payments can vary with the possibility of advances for certain work.

The cash flow on costs is reasonably straightforward; it is possible that you will have more trouble with the calculations regarding income. Let's take it line by line in Figure 1.1.

Subscription income
From a cash flow point of view this can be very important. Consider the possibility of your initial mailings attracting 1500 founder subscribers before publication: say your subscription rate is £20, then you will have £30,000 nestling in the bank before you start, which is comforting. Of course, the cost of getting these subscribers can be very high; we discuss this in more detail in Chapter 2 on marketing. It may be worth pointing out here that this subscription money is held on behalf of your subscribers who become your creditors (people to whom you owe money) and it is a liability on your balance sheet. On the other hand, it's great for cash flow.

16   Publishing Your Own Specialist Magazine

Newsagent sales

You will find that your newsagent distributor will want to pay you on a staged system of payments. This is customary although the amounts and when they are paid will vary. This staged method of payments is, to a certain extent, applied to cover the spread of payments and magazine returns from the various wholesalers.

A common system of payment from the distributor is as follows: 50 per cent after 30 days, 25 per cent after 60 days, and a further 25 per cent after 90 days. Bear in mind that, with a monthly magazine, there will be a return deduction after 60 days and this will have an effect on every month's payment. To begin with, your return will be high for the reasons we have discussed earlier, but this should settle down to a consistent percentage after the first few issues.

Other trade sales and advertising

These are easier to plan as you will probably set a 30-day credit limit for UK customers and a 60-day limit for overseas customers. If you take your total revenue column away from the total cost column you will notice some quite dramatic peaks and troughs in your cash flow. It is the troughs you need to cater for in your initial funding; you must be able to support what in the jargon is called rather euphemistically 'negative cash flow'. Unless you have great personal financial resources or are being subsidised by an organisation you will probably need a bank and an accountant.

Banks and accountants

You will need the services of an accountant to help you run your business, particularly in the delicate early stages of its growth. It will probably be necessary to bring an accountant into the planning stages of the magazine. If you intend to raise capital either by means of a loan or an overdraft from the bank, you will need a *business plan* and it is as well, unless you have a sound financial background, to have an accountant to help you with the figures.

Your business plan should consist of a description of your magazine proposal.

- What will the content of the magazine be?
- What is the competition?
- What is the market?
- How do you intend to produce your product, and sell it?

Specialist Magazine X	Nov	Dec	Jan	Feb	Mar	Apr	May	Jun	Jul	Aug	Sep	Oct	Total
Rent, rates, insurance	1550	1550	1550	1550	1550	1550	1550	1550	1550	1550	1550	1550	18600
Salaries, Nat Insurance	5300	5300	5300	5300	5300	5300	5300	5300	5300	5300	5300	5300	63600
Expenses	500	500	500	500	500	500	500	500	500	500	500	500	6000
Postage and packing	100	100	100	100	100	100	100	100	100	100	100	100	1200
Telephone/Fax	125	125	125	125	125	125	125	125	125	125	125	125	1500
Accountancy	3000						2000						5000
Travel	300	300	300	300	300	300	300	300	300	300	300	1000	4300
Bank charges	1500	1500	1500	1500	1500	1500	1500	1500	1500	1500	1500	1500	18000
Freelance staff	1800	1800	1800	1800	1800	1800	1800	1800	1800	1800	1800	1800	21600
Sundry	250	250	250	250	250	250	250	250	250	250	250	250	3000
Stationery	2500	1500	250	50	50	50	50	50	50	50	50	50	4700
Total Overheads	16925	12925	11675	11475	11475	11475	13475	11475	11475	11475	11500	12175	147500

Figure 1.2. *Typical overheads for a small business*

18   **Publishing Your Own Specialist Magazine**

The bank will also be interested in your qualifications and background as well as the credentials of any partners you may have. The figures should show profit and loss and cash flow predictions for the first and second years, given that it may take more than a year to show a firm growth pattern and 'positive cash flow'. These will be similar to the sheet illustrated on page 10 but you will also need another set of vital figures to complete the picture – the overheads of your business.

Figure 1.2 shows a typical set of overheads for a small business which, although not comprehensive, should give some idea of the principal categories to be covered. These overheads must be set against the profits from the direct costs/revenue from the magazine.

Your choice of bank will in the first instance be one of the high street banks who have all geared themselves up in recent years to the needs of small businesses. For overdrafts and small loans of up to, say, £30,000–£40,000, they will almost always require security and an investment from you in terms of hard cash before they undo the purse strings.

If you require larger amounts of money or have little security then you will probably have to look for some form of venture capital which will require a high return on investment. Your financial plan, carefully prepared, will tell you how much you want and when. This is essential information for both you and your prospective banker and/or backer.

You will have to run the mechanics of your business and you will need someone to look after your bookkeeping, VAT returns, PAYE and so on. Depending on the size of your business, there are a number of ways to tackle this. If your business is small, your accountant will no doubt be able to look after all this for you or help you to find a part-time bookkeeper.

If you have access to a computer, there are a number of excellent software programs available which provide bookkeeping facilities. With sufficient time and enthusiasm it is possible to operate a bookkeeping computer system yourself or train an assistant (wife, husband, partner?). This will also save you a useful sum of money (excluding the cost of computer and software).

Credit control

Although you will expect advertisers and trade purchasers of your magazine to pay within the credit limits you set, some customers will be less than prompt. It is essential to keep a

Financial Planning 19

careful check on payments being made to you, and for someone to chase invoices that are not paid within the agreed period.

In the first instance you might want to chase them up with a letter, followed by a telephone call. This can sometimes be difficult because, although you want your money, you also need the customer's repeat business. However, be polite yet persistent and make sure that you have a chosen course of action for those who seem determined not to pay.

Going through a solicitor and the courts is another option for large, outstanding debts but there are other, less expensive ways of applying pressure. A number of companies offer a debt collection service; some also offer an insurance system which covers bad debts. Dun and Bradstreet, for example, will, for a percentage of the invoice value, undertake debt collection on an international basis as well as obtain credit checks for you on potential customers whose creditworthiness you are unsure about. It is also possible to take action on debts through the small claims section of the county court which is a fairly simple and inexpensive way of recovering money that is owed to you.

Chapter 2
Marketing and PR

You are no doubt aware of the truism that the principal cause of most new business failure is insufficient marketing. This is only too true of magazine publishing. It is not enough to produce what you think is an excellent, much needed magazine and push it out on to an unsuspecting public. You need to advertise, not just at the launch of your magazine but also periodically throughout its life. However, marketing entails more than just advertising and promotion.

The four Ps

An easy way to remember what marketing is and does is the four P method: Product, Price, Place, Promotion. This highlights the most important marketing considerations in any business.

Product
It goes without saying that you must have the right product, which means you must think carefully about the market you are aiming for and what it wants. The editorial approach, the coverage and the physical look of the magazine are all important considerations. Remember too that you will almost certainly have more than one market to consider. As well as the eventual reader you will also need to bear in mind the wholesaler's and retailer's requirements and the needs of your advertisers who may, in terms of financial contribution, be as important as your readership. There will almost certainly be conflicting priorities when the magazine is being conceived and it is important that you should keep the interests of the market in view when working out solutions to these problems.

Price
Price has a great deal to do with the product, of course, but again, market considerations are vital. When arriving at a price for the magazine you will need to look at some important factors. How much is it actually costing you to produce the product? What gross profit do you need to make, and therefore how much do

you need to charge? This will give you an economic price. Now put those considerations to one side and try to arrive at a market price.

What will the market pay for your product? This price could be arrived at by looking at the prices of competitive magazines, or by relating the size, shape and weight of your magazine to others on sale – sometimes a useful guide – but perhaps the most important question still is, what will your readers pay?

It may be, for example, that you are producing a magazine which is similar in style to the competition but, because your magazine is new your print run is low and consequently the unit cost is high. There is no point in trying to sell at your economic price because your potential readers have a price in mind that they will pay for that kind of magazine. They will neither know nor care that you arrived at the higher price you are charging, not because you are profiteering but because your costs are high. You will have to charge the price that is perceived to be right by the market.

The relationship of cost to price is still important to you, however, and you will have to find a way to make the margin you need while charging the market price.

Check out the cover prices charged for the wide diversity of magazines on sale. You will notice that very few cost more than £2.50 but that some of the magazines with the lowest cover prices have more pages and more colour than others. You will also see that the more magazines there are in a particular subject area, the lower the prices tend to be.

Once you move away from consumer (general) magazines the market price philosophy still applies but perhaps with rather different effect and, particularly with academic and learned journals, you will find that the market is prepared to pay quite high sums for subscriptions.

The relationship of cover price to subscription is important. In the US, where readers are more subscription-orientated than in Britain, magazines tend to have a much lower subscription price than the total annual cover price. Sometimes magazines in the United States can offer 35-45 per cent reductions on the cover price for a subscription. The economics of subscriptions have been discussed in Chapter 1 but these American publishers have obviously calculated the benefits of attracting large numbers of subscribers, and the discounts they are offering are made up for by the cash in hand (or rather in the bank!) benefits.

In the UK this tends to be less common and quite often subscriptions will be more expensive than the total annual cover

22   **Publishing Your Own Specialist Magazine**

price. It depends very much whether your magazine is likely to be subscribed to and what your subscription-handling costs are.

Place

It is vital to get your magazine in the right place to achieve sales. This 'place' could be a variety of outlets; they all need to be examined and the ways of approaching each one carefully planned. You will probably reach the most usual and easily accessible outlets through a distributor. However, once your magazine arrives at the newsagent, it has to be displayed on the shelves somewhere and you will need to make sure, particularly in the case of the large multiples such as WH Smith, Menzies etc, that your magazine is properly 'positioned'. You will, for example, probably want to be among magazines of a similar type, but there can be more than one group to put your magazine in, and you may want to find a specific slot. This is something you can only try to influence; the shops themselves have the final say, of course, and in the multiple chains there are carefully worked out plans for what goes where on the shelves.

You will need to investigate all the other ways of making sure that your magazine is in the right place. Are there exhibitions that deal with your subject? Then your magazine should be there. Can you find other retail outlets that don't normally carry magazines but whose customers would be interested? If your readers meet in small or large groups on a regular basis can you find someone to make sure the magazine is on sale? Remember, if your magazine isn't in the right place it won't sell.

Promotion

People have got to be made aware that your magazine exists and promotion covers the many ways and means that can be used to obtain that all-important visibility.

You will want to promote your magazine to readers, advertisers and, sometimes, even the retailing staff who sell it. The many ways of promoting your magazine to readers include direct mail, press advertising and public relations.

Direct mail

Direct mail is particularly useful if you want to start building or increasing your subscriber list. But before you do anything you must find out where your prospective subscribers will come from and whether you can obtain their names and addresses. The complexities of this depend very much on the nature of your magazine but you will almost always be able to identify clubs, groups or societies which will have an interest. Some of these will possibly have their own magazine or newsletter but this will not necessarily stop them giving you access to their members – if you pay them, although the charge may not be high. Ideally, you want a set of names and addresses on labels or a disc which you can use to mail direct. This will enable you to send a covering letter with your brochure which will usually increase the response to your mailing.

You will find, however, that more and more of these groups are becoming aware of the value of their membership lists and are increasingly reluctant to let an outsider see them. They may only agree to your approaching their members if they send out your mailing piece. This is better than nothing, of course, but you may be limited to when they are sending their next membership mailing.

You will be able to find the names and addresses of many societies in the *Directory of British Associations* published by CBD Research Ltd. You can also attempt to rent the subscriber list of competitive publications (if they will let you) or publications which have a similar readership. The cost will be relatively high but will enable you to make a 'personalised' approach to these potential customers. You can always put an insert in such magazines which will give you a higher response than simply taking advertising space. An insert is a loose leaflet inserted in each copy.

Producing a brochure about your magazine gives you the opportunity to describe its content and editorial approach, list forthcoming articles and the names of some of its more important or interesting contributors. You can also show one or two specimen pages and generally build up the profile of the publication. The brochure, if you are using it to attract subscribers, must have a good, clear, easy-to-complete order form, offering as many ways to buy as you can, making it as easy as possible for the reader. A typical order form specimen is shown in Figure 2.1.

Offering credit cards is an essential sales aid these days and you must apply for 'Mail Order Status' as a credit card retailer as soon as possible in advance of your very first mailings. To become a mail order retailer (which is what in fact you will need to be to take subscriptions) is slightly more difficult than becoming a conventional retailer; it puts the credit card company at more risk as the transaction is done at a distance. You must contact the major companies, which these days probably mean ACCESS/

24   Publishing Your Own Specialist Magazine

Tick box required. Save up to 33%.

☐ 1 Year – 13 issues – £19.95 (27% discount)

☐ 2 Years – 26 issues – £39.00 (30% discount)

☐ 3 Years – 39 issues – £57.18 (33% discount)

Name: _____

Address: _____

_____

_____ Post code: _____

☐ I enclose a cheque for ☐ £19.95 ☐ £39.00 ☐ £57.18
Cheque made payable to Get Rich Quick Ltd or debit my
credit card ☐ Barclaycard ☐ Access ☐ Amex

No ☐☐☐☐☐☐☐☐☐☐☐☐☐☐☐☐☐☐☐

Expiry date .... Signed ....

The above offers apply to UK and Eire only. Air Mail Europe:
£30.95, Rest of the World £42.95 (Annual Rate)

I understand that no refunds can be given for subscriptions cancelled before expiry.

Figure 2.1. *Specimen order form*

Mastercard, VISA/Barclaycard and American Express, although
the latter tends to be chary about new, small mail order retailers
and also tends to deduct a larger percentage charge. The charge
levied by the other two companies can be anywhere between 3
and 5 per cent of your order value. Apply early and persevere
with your application, as you will lose business without having
this facility.

Remember also when you are planning your brochure that
there are other uses you could put it to to save on cost, if it is
carefully designed. With a little adaptation the brochure can be
used when you are mailing your advertisers, and quite possibly
for an initial mailing to wholesalers and retailers. Identify the
copy that will need to be changed at the design stage and make
sure that all this is kept in one area which can easily be altered
by the printer, if you want to save on cost. If you are printing a
brochure in four colours make sure, if you can, that all copy to be
changed appears in an area of single colour so that you need only
make one plate change. Your designer or printer will be able to
help you with this.

If you are able to personalise your brochure with a covering letter then always do so. This gives you the flexibility to tailor your message to different audiences if you wish and to make special offers to particular groups if you feel it would be advantageous. You can, for instance, offer a lower subscription price or an extra free copy for the first year's subscription, or your letter can simply expound the merits of the magazine and point out its particular benefits to that particular customer as one of a highly valued society etc.

For mailing a number of different lists, think about coding the order form of your brochure or leaflet so that you can identify responses when orders are sent in. This would entail putting a number or letter code on those brochures which are going to the different mailings. The printer of your mailing piece could do this for you without a great deal of additional expense. You will then need to make sure that the right brochures go out to the correct lists. It is of great value to see which lists your response is coming from and to go back to those highly responsive sectors of your mailing, and mail them again.

Mailing for subscribers is likely to be an expensive but highly productive means of promotion. In the beginning you will be selling a magazine that has not yet or only recently been published. As time goes on you will be able to use the magazine itself as a trawl for subscribers and will want to advertise for them in selected, if not all, issues in an attempt to convert your casual, issue-by-issue buyers into subscribers. Your initial mailings will need to contain a good deal of reassurance for the potential buyer, and if you can obtain quotes from satisfied subscribers or personalities who might be known to your prospective audience or whose views they would value, then try to do so.

Although relatively expensive, the advantages of the mail shot are that the outlay and the return are known, measurable quantities and, unlike many other methods of promotion, you can usually see quite clearly what has worked.

Be sure to cost out your mailing before you implement it and work out your potential return on investment. The question people always ask is 'If I carry out mailing X or insert Y, what percentage response am I going to get?' There are no hard-and-fast answers to this question as so much depends on the list you are using, the mailing piece, the magazine you are selling, the offer you are making, the time of the year you mail it etc. Rule of thumb percentages which might help as a rough guide are as follows. For an insert in a magazine, the average response is

26 **Publishing Your Own Specialist Magazine**

unlikely to be more than 0.5 per cent. On an average mailing with covering letter and brochure the response to a reasonable list is unlikely to be more than 1.5 per cent. Any mailing that exceeds a 5 per cent response is extraordinary.

Your mail-out to potential advertisers will probably need to carry more detailed information on the kind of readers you are going to attract, their particular characteristics, percentage breakdown by age, even a demographic breakdown if you can, together with the rate card (cost of advertisements) and technical specifications for the magazine. It may also need to be a more specific, targeted letter which will not be looking for an immediate response but will create an opening for a follow-up telephone call or visit.

Press advertising

As a general rule, press advertising is used as a circulation booster. It is used most often by magazines, not in isolation but to back up a specific promotional drive which the distributors are mounting through their wholesaler/retailer network. What happens is that the publisher and distributor agree to mount a circulation drive on a particular issue. This might tie in with a special editorial feature or some other promotional hook. They will then come up with a plan for promoting that issue which might involve a number of different promotional activities – PR, point of sale (both of which are discussed below) and press advertising. This promotion would then be taken to the wholesaler to gain his support in taking more copies of the magazine, so that the increased media visibility is backed up by increased visibility at the point of sale.

To use press advertising on its own without building it into a well-thought out promotional campaign is likely to be wasteful. The exception (and in this business there *is* an exception to every rule) might be where an advertisement is placed for a specific reason and there are firm indications that there is going to be a satisfactory return on the money or an image boost of some kind. Press advertising works in the main through repetition (tell your potential advertisers!) and magazine budgets are unlikely to support the large expenditure required to make them work as a stand-alone, promotional activity.

Point-of-sale material

This is rarely the most important feature of magazine promotion, simply because the outlets where magazines tend to be sold are crowded and leave little room for showcards, posters and other point-of-sale material. Consequently, smaller point-of-sale items are more commonly used. Shelf strips and 'talkers' (small, shelf-mounted messages) even 'wobblers' (messages mounted on a spring or springy plastic which, yes you've guessed, wobble when they are touched) are all used but again, usually in conjunction with a coordinated promotion which is part of a planned promotion programme. 'Bolt-ons' (an item stuck to the outside of the magazine like a feeler gauge for a car magazine or a record on a 'teeny' magazine) are a common one-off promotion, as are plastic magazine sleeve wrappers which feature a promotional message and are fairly inexpensive to produce.

Public relations

The great thing about this form of promotion is that it's free – or almost. You can employ a professional PR company to promote your magazine on a regular basis or for a specific issue or campaign, but this can become expensive and there is a lot you can do in-house without a great deal of knowledge or experience. You will probably want to publicise your first 'launch' issue, but after this you must always consider the PR advantages of each issue and the stories (or photographs) within the issue as the possible basis of a story to the press.

First of all, let us look at who the press are and how to reach them. There are a number of publications which give the names, addresses, telephone and fax numbers of journalists and editors in the media. One of the best known is *PIMS Media Directory* published by Pims London. This is updated on a monthly basis and although it is not cheap (an annual subscription is about £200) the information is invaluable and the cost can easily be recouped by one substantial feature for your magazine. Some libraries carry this and similar publications.

The listings in the guide are presented by printed media, national and provincial newspapers, dailies, weeklies and free sheets; national technical and specialist magazines (remember that it would also be useful to get your own magazine listed in these directories – the listing is usually free); and national and local radio and television. Within these sections there are also subject listings (for example, women's interest, aviation, gardening, antiques etc) with the names of those journalists specifically interested in the subject for their particular paper, radio station or programme. National newspapers will have a complete listing of all their senior journalists: diarists, features editors, picture editors and so on. This is invaluable if you want to direct your approach to the right person, as you must.

Whom you approach with your story will depend on a number of factors, but remember that although your magazine may not be dealing with controversial or, on the face of it, newsworthy subjects, it is always possible to find something of interest to the media.

It may be useful to adopt the 'so what' attitude to your potential ideas about a story. OK, so you are starting a magazine on keeping pet goldfish and you want to get some publicity. If you send out a press release that is worded as follows you can understand the journalist's 'so what' reaction.

PRESS RELEASE

This month a new magazine for people who keep goldfish as pets is to be launched. The magazine will deal with all aspects of goldfish ownership for the amateur and professional. Published by Fishy Publications it will retail at 95p etc, etc.

Unless you hit a devoted goldfish owner/journalist this is destined for the bin. You might have a bit more success if you look for something to 'hang the story on to', a short but potentially interesting statement which can act as bait to lead on to your main thrust. How about:

PRESS RELEASE

The disastrous consequences of stress in the modern world, heart disease, strokes etc, can be overcome by the smallest and cheapest pet – a goldfish. Over five million people in this country benefit from the health-giving properties of this simple creature which lowers the blood pressure and relaxes those who watch it. The editor of *'Keeping Goldfish' a new magazine out on 23 November* says . . . and so on.

This is more likely to get a journalist somewhere to stop and think that this might make an interesting or amusing piece. Sending out your story as a press release is the conventional way to get your message over. Make sure you are concise and to the point. It is usually best, although not essential, to keep to one side of an A4 sheet and use double-spaced typing. Be clear about where the reader can obtain further information with a telephone number and so on. If you have a photograph (the same 'so what' principles apply - don't be boring) then attach it to the release. Remember to caption the photograph separately and don't paper-clip it to the release. It will mark the photo.

You need not necessarily use press-release paper, a letter will do. You can, of course, always telephone the journalist direct but remember that you have even less time to put your story over this way. It is usually best to send your press release first and follow it up with a telephone call. Be prepared for rejection and off-handedness; you are just one of many trying to place a story and, unless you have a really hot piece of news, you may have to work hard to get your message across. However, you can sometimes be surprised at the take-up of even a rather slender story if it is well presented.

The growth of local radio in recent years has meant an ever-increasing need on the broadcasters' part to fill air time, and books and magazines have always been a trawling ground for stories and personalities to interview and sit in on phone-ins etc. It may be possible for you or your editor to be accepted by your local station as their resident expert on whatever the magazine subject is (and this can apply to other media) so that you are pulled in for any associated news story and, of course, the magazine is mentioned each time.

Television is rather more difficult to get to as there are fewer TV stations and their programme output tends to allow less time for the magazine or feature format programme. However, all TV stations have these slots and if you think you have an interesting story to tell, it is certainly worth trying.

Remember that marketing is an integral part of producing and selling your magazine. It should be planned and thought about as far ahead of your launch as possible and every year you should devise some promotional activities to keep your product before the readers.

Chapter 3
The Role of the Editor

The editor's job in a specialist magazine may have to encompass many of the other activities described in this book and in a small company the editor may also be the publisher or the managing director. In this chapter we look at the editor's specific function of producing the right words and pictures, to the right length, and *on time*. The importance of these last two words for a magazine editor is paramount. The editor's job in a regularly produced magazine is a vital part of a closely interlocked chain of events which ends with the reader opening the magazine. The editor will have a set of dates in his diary around which life revolves and it is usually the editor who has to make sure that all those involved in producing the magazine adhere to those dates.

Content and quality

The role of an editor in a new publication is paramount. It is the editor who should give the magazine its 'voice', and dictate its content and quality. Although the editor may not necessarily be a specialist or enthusiast in the subject covered by the magazine (some of the best ones aren't), he will, of course, need to acquaint himself very thoroughly with the magazines' area of activity. Visits to clubs or societies, conferences and exhibitions, and getting to know the personalities involved, are essential to acquiring the correct editorial tone and to the magazine's approach. All this needs to be undertaken well before the magazine gets under way and the editor may well need a year to prepare before the first issue.

Your editor may have had previous experience of working on a similar magazine either as an editor or a writer, in which case you have a flying start. If your editor (who may, of course, be you, dear reader) is an enthusiast but has no previous experience of editing a magazine, then be careful. The history of commercial, specialist magazines is littered with the corpses of titles started by enthusiasts who underestimated the job of editor. On the other hand, there are a number of shining examples of commercial magazines edited by amateurs which have become vast money-earners or highly respected in their field. This is especially satisfying for the enthusiastic entrepreneur when you consider that established publishing companies spend fortunes on market research trying to identify new markets and new titles.

If your magazine is the outcome of an interest you have or arises out of an organisation with which you are connected, and you have had no previous editorial experience, there are a number of books and courses which would be of use to you.

Editing skills

There are some basic skills which an editor must have and the ability to correct a manuscript in a way that can be understood by a typesetter or printer is essential. Some typical editorial correction marks are shown in Figure 3.1.

Format and approach

Having decided on the content and tone of the magazine, it will be necessary to devise a format. How many articles will appear in each issue? What features will appear on a regular basis? Letters page, editorial comment, profiles, news section, book reviews and so on? Any regular publication benefits from having a framework of items which appear in every issue and often on particular pages. It's reassuring for the reader to turn to his favourite item, apart from making the editorial problem of filling every issue easier by establishing this structure and cutting down on the number of decisions that need to be made.

The editor, of course, has to decide how the magazine will deal with its topic and this decision is normally taken at an early planning stage. Whether based on market research or just plain 'hunch', the style or approach of the magazine needs to be established. Take any magazine topic and there are always many ways to tackle the editorial content. The initial planning which we looked at in the first chapter will have established the framework for this but it is the editor's job to make sure that it is carried through. It is not much good, for example, having decided on a high-priced magazine, with high production values, if the text is written in a down-market way. Think of a combination of the *Sun* newspaper's editorial style and *The Times*' layout etc, and you can imagine how strange this would look.

32   Publishing Your Own Specialist Magazine

Mark in margin		Meaning	Corresponding mark in text
British Standard BS 5261	Older style *		
/	/	Correction is concluded	None
⅄	New matter followed by /	Insert in text the matter indicated in margin	⅄
ᶁ	ᶁ	Delete	Strike through characters to be deleted / ⊢⊣
ᶁ̂	ᶁ̂	Delete and close up	
⊘	stet	Leave as printed	. . . . under characters to remain
⊔	ital	Change to italic	—— under characters to be altered
══	sc	Set in or change to small capitals	—— under characters to be altered
≡	caps	Set in or change to capital letters	≡≡ under characters to be altered
≡	c & sc	Set in or use capitals for initial letters and small capitals for rest of words	≡≡ under initial letters and —— under the rest of the words
∿	bold	Change to bold type	∿ under characters to be altered
≢	lc	Change to lower case	Encircle characters to be altered
4	rom	Change to roman type	Encircle character to be altered
⊗	wf	Wrong fount. Replace by letter of correct fount	Encircle character to be altered
↱	⤴	Invert type	Encircle character to be altered
X	X	Change damaged character(s)	Encircle character(s) to be altered
⅄	under character (eg 1/)	Substitute or insert character(s) under which this mark is placed, in 'superior' position	/ through character or ⅄ where required
⌒	enclosing ligature or diphthong required	Use ligature (eg ﬃ) or diphthong (eg œ)	⊢⊣ through letters to be altered
Write out separate letters	Write out separate letters followed by /	Substitute separate letters for ligature or diphthong	/ through ligature or diphthong to be altered
⌣	⌣	Close up – delete space between characters or words	⌣ linking characters
Υ	#	Insert space	⅄ or Υ
⟩ ⟨	#	Insert space between lines or paragraphs	⟩ between lines to be spaced
( )	less #	Reduce space between lines	(connecting lines to be closed up

* Old habits die hard, and you still find these symbols in use.

The Role of the Editor   33

Mark in margin		Meaning	Corresponding mark in text
British Standard BS 5261	Older style *		
Y	letter ⋕	Add space between letters or characters	⏌⏌⏌⏌ between tops of characters requiring space
⊔⊓	trs	Transpose	⊔⊓ between characters or words, numbered when necessary
[ ]	centre	Place in centre of line	Indicate position with ⌐ ⌐
⊰	☐	Indent	⊰
⊰	⊰	Move matter to right	⊰ at left side of group to be moved or ⟼
⊱	⊱	Move matter to left	⊱ at right side of group to be moved or ⟻
	take over	Take over character(s) or line to next line, column or page	[
	take back	Take back character(s) or line to previous line, column or page	]
⏋⎽⏌	raise	Raise lines	⟍⟍ over lines to be moved; ⏋⎽⏌ under lines to be moved
⎽⏋⎽	lower	Lower lines	⏋⎽ over lines to be moved; ↓ under lines to be moved
‖	‖	Correct the vertical alignment	‖
═	═	Straighten lines	═ through lines to be straightened
⎽⏋	np or ⚶	Begin a new paragraph	[before first word of new paragraph
⌒	run on	No fresh paragraph	⌒ between paragraphs
	spell out	Spell out the abbreviation or figure in full	Encircle words or figures to be altered
	out see copy	Insert omitted portion of copy. The relevant section of the setting copy should be returned with the proof, the omitted portion being clearly indicated	⋋
⟩	⟩/	Substitute or insert comma	/ through character or ⋋ where required
⦂	⦂/	Substitute or insert semi-colon	/ through character or ⋋ where required
⊙	⊙	Substitute or insert full stop	/ through character or ⋋ where required

Figure 3.1. *Symbols for correcting proofs*

Dealing with contributors

Once this has been thrashed out and the first half-dozen issues planned, if only in rough, the relevant contributors need to be chosen. Most magazines use freelance writers who are commissioned to produce regular or occasional articles. In the beginning you will be looking for writers who are already writing in the same field or indeed specialists or enthusiasts who, although they are not professional writers, can put together an article which can be knocked into shape by the editor.

In all this you will be working to a budget which has been previously agreed. It is important to keep a tight rein on the editorial budget for each issue. This will include all fees paid to contributors and may or may not include the editor's salary or fee. You will have agreed fees for regularly contributed columns, which will be agreed between the editor and the writer. There are National Union of Journalist rates for payment for wordage (the number of words in a piece) but so much depends on the nature of your publication that it is difficult to give exact guidelines.

The editor will have to negotiate fees, depending on the writer or photographer and what they have to supply. It must be clearly established what the subject of the piece is to be, how many words it should contain and whether pictures or illustrations are to be supplied.

It is usual to pay for contributions on publication or 30 days after; although advances are sometimes made this is not usual. Out-of-pocket expenses need to be contained and some prior agreement about the scale of these should be agreed in advance. Any expenses relating to travel or research costs are best wrapped up in the total fee if at all possible, avoiding any grey areas of cost.

Ideally, the relationship between editor and writers is based on trust and mutual respect. The life of a full-time freelance writer is often somewhat precarious and the editor who establishes a good relationship with his writers and treats them fairly will find this pays dividends in terms of well-written copy, delivered on time, and helpful suggestions for future pieces. Contracts are rare and usually unnecessary, unless you are arranging for an article or feature which is to be a permanent fixture in the magazine.

House style

It is useful for every contributor to receive written instructions setting out the magazine's 'house style' and the way material

The Role of the Editor   35

should be presented. Although not absolutely essential it is useful if the contributors deliver articles in a way that makes them easy to sub-edit and provide instructions for the typesetter. An editor may specify that all copy should be double- or triple-spaced (a common requirement to allow for additions and corrections to the copy) and that the typed measure is limited to a width which allows a wide column for notes, instructions to the designer about pictures, and so on.

It is also a good idea to lay down simple rules for the way words are written. For example, numbers can be spelt out or written as figures. An instruction on this might be: 'one to ten spell out, 11 and over use numerals'. A possible exception to this is where numbers might be spelled out for effect as in 'thousands of pounds were squandered on the magazine'. The way dates, measurements, capitals, quotes and abbreviations are expressed can all be covered in an explanatory document of advice for authors.

It might also be useful in the same document to spell out the terms of your agreement with contributors: when you pay; what happens if the material that's supplied isn't up to the standard you require; whether you expect photographs and illustrations to be provided by the writer, and so on. It may also be possible to provide a brief rundown in general terms on what kind of articles you would like to publish in the magazine.

You will find that this kind of document is, apart from anything else, useful to send to the many hopeful contributors you will probably attract when the magazine is being published regularly.

You might also like to cover yourself regarding the question of libel, which in some areas is an increasingly difficult problem, pointing out that it is the author's responsibility to ensure that no actionable material is published. In law it is your responsibility as the publisher to ensure this but there is no harm in getting your writers to think seriously about the consequences of their purple prose.

Once the magazine is under way you will find that unsolicited articles will be sent or proposals for articles made. The editor will need to have a policy on these; some magazines have a regular statement on the contents page to the effect that unsolicited manuscripts are welcome if accompanied by a stamped addressed envelope and no responsibility is accepted by the publisher. It is, of course, a way of 'acquiring articles although, depending on your editorial standards, the chances of getting good quality copy this way are likely to be a little hit or miss.

MILITARY ILLUSTRATED

① OFC

② OFC ③

④ ⑤

⑥ ⑦

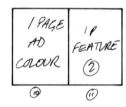
⑧ ⑨ ⑩ ⑪ ⑫ ⑬

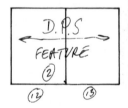

⑭ ⑮ ⑯ ⑰ ⑱ ⑲

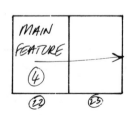
⑳ ㉑ ㉒ ㉓

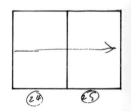
㉔ ㉕

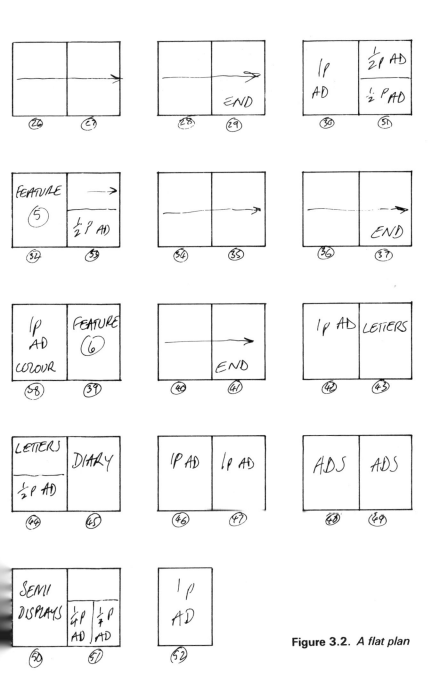

Figure 3.2. A flat plan

Editing copy

Once an article is delivered the nuts and bolts part of the editor's job begins, sub-editing the piece and marking it up for the typesetter. In larger companies this may be looked after by an assistant to the editor, but very often the editor does it for the good of his soul. The article will need to be read and all the facts verified, the spelling and punctuation checked and made to conform to editorial house style. It should then be checked to make sure it fits the intended space and marked up from an editorial point of view for the typesetter, with capitalisation, underlining and so on clearly marked. Most editors will work to a page-by-page layout of the magazine (like the one shown in Figure 2) which will give the exact position of each article on the page and the position of advertisements.

Although making sure the artwork for the advertisements has been received may not be the editor's responsibility, he will probably find that the job of planning any particular issue will involve positioning the advertisements with, of course, the advice of the person selling the advertising, who will in some cases have to incorporate specific requests made by advertisers, for particular pages or positions on pages.

Schedules

As we mentioned at the outset, an editor's diary is his bible and among the skills of commissioning the articles and shaping the magazine, working with writers and photographers, and keeping to a tight financial budget is a skill which is akin to juggling a number of plates without dropping any. Once in full publication, the editor of a monthly magazine, for example, might be sending one issue off for printing, checking the bromides and colour proofs of the following issue, subbing and checking galley proofs of the issue after that as well as commissioning articles for two or three issues in advance of those. At any one time the editor will be involved at some stage of production with at least four different issues. It can become confusing, and the ability to think on one's feet is useful.

Page plans and proofs

Once the copy has been prepared to the editor's satisfaction, the designer and editor will usually meet to discuss the editor's ideas for the issue and work out a page plan. The editor may provide

The Role of the Editor   39

the designer with some rough ideas on paper and discuss such matters as the treatment of photographs and illustrations, the prominence to be given to this or that feature and any other special requirements. They will also need to take into account the pages which will contain advertising and where they will fall in that particular issue. The editor will then have the task of editing his articles if necessary to fit the available space, to avoid any costly editing after typesetting.

Once this has been done and the manuscript has been 'cast off' (not a knitting term, but the jargon for making sure that the words fit the available space) and 'marked up' (all the type and type sizes specified) it will be sent off to the typesetter for setting. When the typesetting has been returned the designer will often make a 'rough paste up' of the uncorrected galleys, making minor amendments to the layout, sizing pictures and illustrations. At the same time the editor will be proofreading the typesetting (ie checking it for spelling errors and inconsistencies of type). It is possible to do all this via desk-top publishing which is described in Chapter 5 on production.

The designer will then paste down all the material as camera-ready copy (CRC), size up the photographs and return the completed CRC to the editor for final checking before it goes off to the printer. It is essential that any changes are made at this stage. Alterations made after the printer has started work become expensive, and *very* expensive if four-colour separations are involved. There is a psychological tendency not to look really hard at artwork before it goes off to the printer but start to see alterations on the printed proof.

When the proofs come back from the printer the editor will need to check that they contain everything that is on the artwork. Although there should be no difference, be warned – things do fall off artwork, printers are capable of putting photographs (which are often not pasted down if they need to be made to a different size) in upside down, back to front and so on. So check carefully but avoid changes unless absolutely necessary.

Editor and designer will probably want to pay particular attention to any colour proofs. There is a possibility at this stage to 'colour correct' the colour proofs and ask for colours to be made stronger or weaker or changed in some way to achieve the effect you require. The colour proofs will normally be supplied separately from the black and white ones.This is because they are proofed with relatively inexpensive proofing plates which allow for the colour work to be remade if required. Minor 'tweaking' of the colour can always be done on the printing machine.

Good PR

Apart from being able to cope with a mass of detail, and withstand the pressure of the ever-present deadlines the ideal editor should be able and confident enough to act as the spokesperson for the magazine. He should be able to stand on public platforms if the occasion arises and make informed comments on the subject that the magazine is involved in or, if required, appear on radio or even television, speaking on behalf of the publication. As discussed in Chapter 2 on marketing and public relations the sales potential of getting the name of your magazine across in the media is great.

To sum up, the editor must be able to get on well with his contributors, have a good eye for detail, be literate and numerate, work well under pressure, be able to make decisions quickly, have some idea about design, know what the reader wants and be able to anticipate the 'fashion' changes of the magazine's subject, and be capable of producing innovative ideas to keep the magazine fresh and maintain reader interest. Sounds easy, doesn't it?

Chapter 4
Design

Vastly improved standards of design over the last 15-18 years have raised the design awareness and expectation of the general public. However specialised your periodical or magazine, it is important that it is attractive and well presented. Even if your magazine is not being sold on the news-stands it is frankly insulting to your reader if your publication is badly designed and presented. Design that enhances your words and pictures need not be expensive. But bad design can transform the most exciting article or feature into a dull or mediocre looking piece that no one will bother to read. On the other hand, the design must be appropriate to the publication. There is little point in using fashionable typefaces and zappy design for a learned journal, for example.

You should be looking for a graphic designer, and it is useful to find someone with experience of magazine layout. Don't be misled into thinking that because you have an eye for design you can do it yourself. It may be that with a publication which requires little illustration or variety in terms of typefaces and styles, the designer would be able to set a grid format, allowing you or your printer to lay out and paste up the publication from this standard format. This would limit the cost to the designer's initial work with perhaps an occasional discussion from time to time when something unusual crops up. However, if you have a high illustrative content and your magazine needs to have reader appeal, then professional design help is essential.

How do I find a designer?

Finding a designer, particularly a good one, can be difficult. Word-of-mouth recommendation is indispensable, but if you have no contacts in the business, there are other ways to find someone suitable apart from using the telephone directory.

Designers or design groups are often listed in the title page credits of a publication. Find a magazine whose style you like and get in touch with the designer. He may be a staff employee, in which case he may have time to take on a freelance job from you.

42   **Publishing Your Own Specialist Magazine**

If you need a full-time designer, why not seek out a number two in a well-designed magazine? Designers and design groups advertise and are listed in Yellow Pages, and the Chartered Society of Designers has a register of designers. Magazines like *Campaign, Creative Review, Design Week* and *Graphics World* are also useful sources of information. If your resources are slender and your publication not too demanding in terms of presentation, then the local art college's final-year graphic students may be a possibility although you may need to watch out for the often fatal combination of inexperience and enthusiasm.

Interviewing and briefing your designer

Finding the right designer and then communicating in non-visual terms your ideas about how the publication should look is not always easy. Ask your prospective designer about his or her previous publication experience and don't be afraid to ask to see what they have previously worked on. Ask if you can see some of their preliminary roughs, which will give you a good idea of how their creative juices flow! Ask about the thinking behind the designs. Good design is largely problem-solving and most graphic designers think logically and enjoy discussing their work. Ask about typography, photographs, layout. Although you may not be the world's greatest authority on the subject you will be able to sense if they have a facility with the tools of their trade. Find out what they know about printing techniques, paper and production generally. Any printer can assure you of the value of a designer who knows about production - he or she can save or lose you money!

Get some feeling for their approach to timing. If your publication is regular and is going to be time-critical, the designer must be able to meet deadlines without skimping the job or throwing a wobbly.

The last and perhaps most important point to discuss is cost. By now you will have some idea about the amount of money you can devote to this activity. Make sure you receive an accurate and detailed quote which covers all aspects of the design and paste up. Do not leave any areas of doubt as to cost. In order for the designer to give you a price for the job, he or she will need to know exactly what is involved, to assess the time it will take. Remember that if you are considering a regular publication you are undertaking to provide the designer with regular work which is highly sought after by most designers or design groups. You

Figure 4.1. *Military Illustrated – Past and Present*

Figures 4.1–4.3. *Different ways to present teaser lines*

Figure 4.2. *Woman's Realm*

Reproduced by kind permission of IPC Magazines Limited.

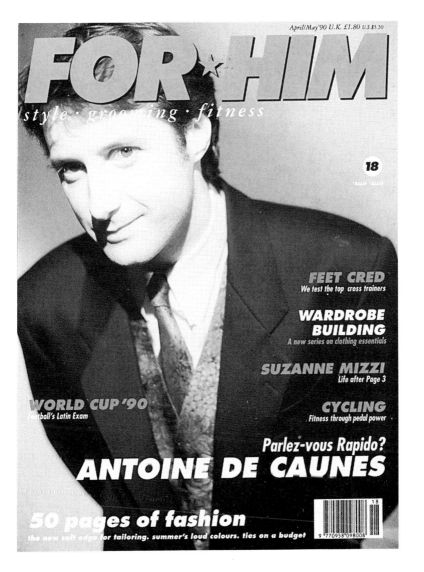

Figure 4.3. *For Him*

Reproduced by kind permission of Tayvale Limited

Figure 4.6. A spread showing imaginative use of a three-column grid Reproduced by kind permission of Tayvale Limited (*For Him*)

should therefore be able to negotiate the price down.

You will probably want to ask him or her to produce a rough design of the publication showing one or two sample spreads, more if you plan on having some variety within the magazine, and a selection of cover designs if this is important to your product.

Designing the cover

If you are considering a commercial publication, particularly if it has to compete on news-stands with the mass of other magazines on show, the design element is even more important. The cover is crucial even if you have a magazine with a targeted readership and casual sales are not thought to be important. Covers always encourage the purchase of those few extra copies which could make a substantial difference over the years. Covers can also reassure the less committed buyer and tell the committed buyer - hey, here I am! The four elements of a cover tend to be:

1. Mast-head
2. Visual
3. Teaser lines
4. Information - price, date etc.

The importance of these elements may vary but some obvious guidelines are as follows.

Mast-head

Your title should usually be at the top left-hand side of the page if there is a choice (look at the way magazines are displayed in newsagents). The typography needs to reflect the magazine's contents if possible, and of course needs to be easily readable at a distance.

Visual

This can be treated in a variety of ways but resist the attempt to try to convey the entire contents of the magazine with a number of different images. Although there are no hard-and-fast rules, one strong image usually works best. If you can afford to have your cover photograph taken specially, this will obviously give you a better chance. However, it can be very expensive if you use a professional photographer. You may be able to select an appropriate photograph from those supplied for the editorial contents of the magazine, or from photographic agencies. Make sure the photograph is carefully selected and that it meets these

44 **Publishing Your Own Specialist Magazine**

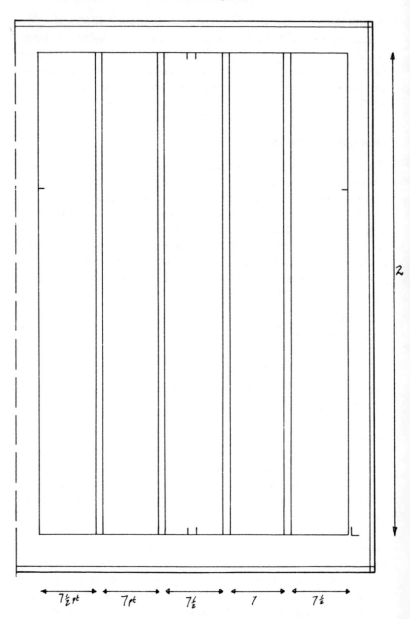

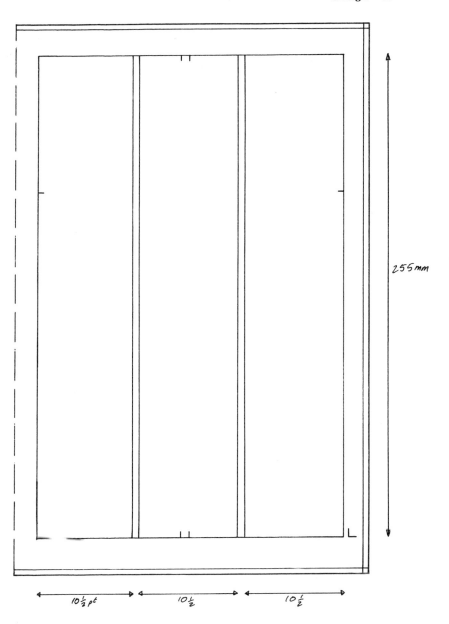

Figures 4.4 and 4.5. *Specimen layout grids*

46 Publishing Your Own Specialist Magazine

basic requirements: is it in focus?; will it stand being blown up to the size of your cover?; is the background in the photograph relevant or can your central image be shown on its own? (This is sometimes called 'cutting out' from the time when the image on the film was cut by hand. Nowadays this can all be done by computer at the origination stage and very complicated cut-outs which were previously considered impossible are now routinely handled.)

Teaser lines

Teaser lines are usually words, or sometimes a picture, which attract the potential reader to the contents of the magazine. You might focus on a lead or more important article with large typography and give less emphasis to subsidiary articles as shown in Figure 4.1. Alternatively, the second cover shown in Figure 4.2 gives equal balance to the teaser lines. Another way of attracting attention to non-editorial features is shown in Figure 4.3. One constant problem with teasers is to make sure that they read clearly, particularly against a four-colour background, or where a line of type runs across a plain background and a four-colour image. Commonly used ways of dealing with this problem are to put the teasers in a box or to put a shadow or black line around the type (as shown in the above mentioned examples).

Publication information

This is not usually a problem as it can be fairly small although the requirement for bar codes (see Chapter 7) means that room needs to be found in the bottom left-hand corner of the front cover.

Text pages

Two typical examples of grids that can be used for a magazine page are shown above in Figures 4.4 and 4.5. If they are followed too slavishly these grid formats can make a dull presentation (which may be perfectly adequate for a learned journal). However, if used intelligently and flexibly, the grid holds the design of the magazine together by creating a framework and giving it a recognisable 'look'.

Figure 4.6 is an example of spreads (open double pages) which shows the use of a grid and exciting and original design. Although top designers are expensive, good design does not necessarily mean great expense and the magazine which is well designed will always have an edge over its competitors.

Chapter 5
Production

Assuming that you have been through the financial planning exercise recommended in Chapter 1, by the time you come to think about producing your magazine, you will have a good idea of the physical shape, size and content you are aiming for. Economics, aesthetics and the right approach to your intended market all come into play here. Unless you can afford to employ a production specialist, either full- or part-time, some knowledge of the various printing processes is useful as well as a basic understanding of other aspects of magazine production, such as paper, typesetting, origination and so on.

I would recommend spending time studying books on the subject as well as talking to printers and other specialists to extend your knowledge of production. However, there is no substitute for applying yourself, confronting any problems that come up, and then asking questions. We deal first with the three basic printing processes you need to be aware of.

Printing

Letterpress

This is the oldest commercial printing process which was, up to 15 years ago, the most common method of producing books and magazines. You may have seen pictures of compositors assembling type in wooden cases (called hot metal setting) which then go off to be inked and paper rolled on to the type.

Letterpress printing is done by the relief method, whereby the inked, raised image is transferred on to paper. It has now largely been replaced by new technologies but you will still find some printers with letterpress machines. You can usually tell if something has been printed letterpress by looking for indentations of type on the reverse side of the paper. Its advantage is that it gives a crisp, clean impression. It is rarely used for commercial publications these days.

Gravure

This is the method that many major magazines, such as women's

48 **Publishing Your Own Specialist Magazine**

magazines and colour supplements, use. In some ways the process is the reverse of letterpress in that instead of being raised, the image is depressed into a metal sheet – the printer's *plate*. Gravure is normally done on a rotary press where the plates are mounted on a cylinder. (In fact, its proper name is rotogravure.) The ink lies in the sunken images, the paper passes over and ink is transferred to it under pressure. Gravure is used for long-run printing and works well with full-colour printing on cheaper papers.

Offset lithography

Usually called litho, this is the most commonly used method of printing magazines. The basic principle is that water and grease do not mix. The plates used on the litho printing machines are smooth, with the areas containing the image treated chemically so that the greasy ink is attracted to them; the surrounding surface is damp so that it doesn't attract the ink. The plate, which is on a roller, transfers, or offsets, the ink image on to a rubber roller which then transfers it on to the paper. It sounds tricky, but this is the way most printed material is produced, and the results in the hands of a good machine-minder can be superb.

Sheet-fed and web offset litho

Your magazine is most likely to be printed litho and there are two quite distinct types of machinery which may handle your job – sheet-fed and web. The reason for using one or other of these methods is connected with the print run and the price that can be obtained. *Sheet-fed* printing, as the term suggests, involves printing on large sheets of paper with, for example, eight pages of the magazine on each sheet (called *to view*) which are printed then taken to a separate process to be folded into pages. Next, the various sections are collated to put all the pages of the magazine in the right order and sent on to the stapling (wire-stitching) process before finally being cut to the exact size on a guillotine.

Web offset machines print on large rolls of paper and the process starts with the paper being fed into one end of these huge, impressive machines; finished magazines come off at the other end. The whole process of printing, heat drying, folding, collating, stitching and guillotining is done 'on line' and is entirely mechanised and computerised. Until a few years ago the use of a web for printing was confined to large print runs, but with the advent of *mini-webs* and other technical sophistications, a smaller print run makes the cost of web printing economical.

Nowadays, if you are considering a print run of more than 20,000 of an average-sized magazine, it is worth comparing the prices for sheet-fed and web printing. One of the costs of web printing is the wastage of paper involved in setting up the machine before it actually prints the job. Once it begins to print it is much quicker to produce finished copies than sheet-fed printing. It is likely that any magazine with a print run in excess of 30,000 copies can be printed cheaper on a web.

Of course, the technicalities involved in all the above can be immense and printing is one of the most jargon-ridden industries (second only to computing). Read what you can, visit a printing works and ask questions.

Paper

This is by far the most expensive element in the production of any magazine. You will find that the cost of paper can be anything from one-third to 50 per cent of the total cost of your job, so it is worth spending a little time understanding it.

You can buy your paper direct from a paper merchant or you can ask your printer to supply it. Although the printer will put a handling charge on the cost of the paper, you may find that this is preferable because:

(a) as the printer is buying in bulk on a regular basis he is receiving a good discount from the merchant some, if not all, of which he will pass on to you;

(b) the printer cannot complain about the quality of the paper he has bought for your job;

(c) holding stocks of paper can tie up valuable cash which could adversely affect your cash flow.

Paper merchants hold substantial quantities of commonly used stock papers and these can be bought 'off the shelf' fairly easily. It is possible to buy 'a making' of paper specifically for your requirements direct from the paper mill but you need to buy very large quantities and you could find that there is a problem matching the stock when you reorder.

Paper comes in different finishes, grades and weights. The *finishes* are many but, for our purposes, there are three worth knowing about. These are cartridge, art and newsprint.

Cartridge paper tends to be bulkier than art paper, weight for weight. Its surface can be fluffy or smooth and on the whole it tends to have less show-through (ie it is less easy to see the print

50 **Publishing Your Own Specialist Magazine**

on the other side of the paper) than art paper and the smoother or coated surface papers are perfectly good for detailed photographic half-tones or colour work.

Art paper, as the word implies, is a very smooth surface paper which is suitable for high quality reproduction. It provides a good surface for colour printing and always looks professional although sometimes, depending on the finished product, it can have an over-glossy and therefore unsubtle appearance.

Newsprint probably needs little explanation. It has a coarse, open surface best suited to black and white photographs, although it can take colour and many newspapers are exploring this to excellent effect. This quality of paper is, however, only usually available in rolls, not as sheets, and is therefore only suitable for web offset printing and consequently longer print runs. If you are printing long runs, newsprint is cheap but unless you want to convey a feeling of immediacy (with a listings magazine, for example) and low price, then it is less suitable for a magazine than the other two types of paper.

Paper merchants, who buy their stocks direct from the paper mill, and then supply printers and their customers, provide a wide variety of *grades* of these types of paper which vary in price and suitability for any particular job. When choosing a paper for your magazine find some printed examples of existing publications which you feel are suitable and then discuss the paper quality with your printer. Alternatively, he will be able to come up with samples which suit your budget and the kind of reproduction quality you want to achieve.

The third variable is the *weight* of the paper which determines its feel and thickness in the hand. The grammes per square metre (gsm) is a standard by which all papers are measured and you will find, for example, a particular make of paper available in a range of weights including 75, 90, 100, 115, 135 and 150 gsm. To give you some idea, many monthly glossy magazines use 100gsm for the bulk of their magazine and 135gsm for the cover.

Typesetting

Although some typesetters still have the traditional hot metal setting, the vast majority are now using various forms of computerised typesetting which are infinitely more flexible. However, it is as well to have a fundamental grasp of the basics of typesetting, particularly when conceiving the original design and layout of your magazine.

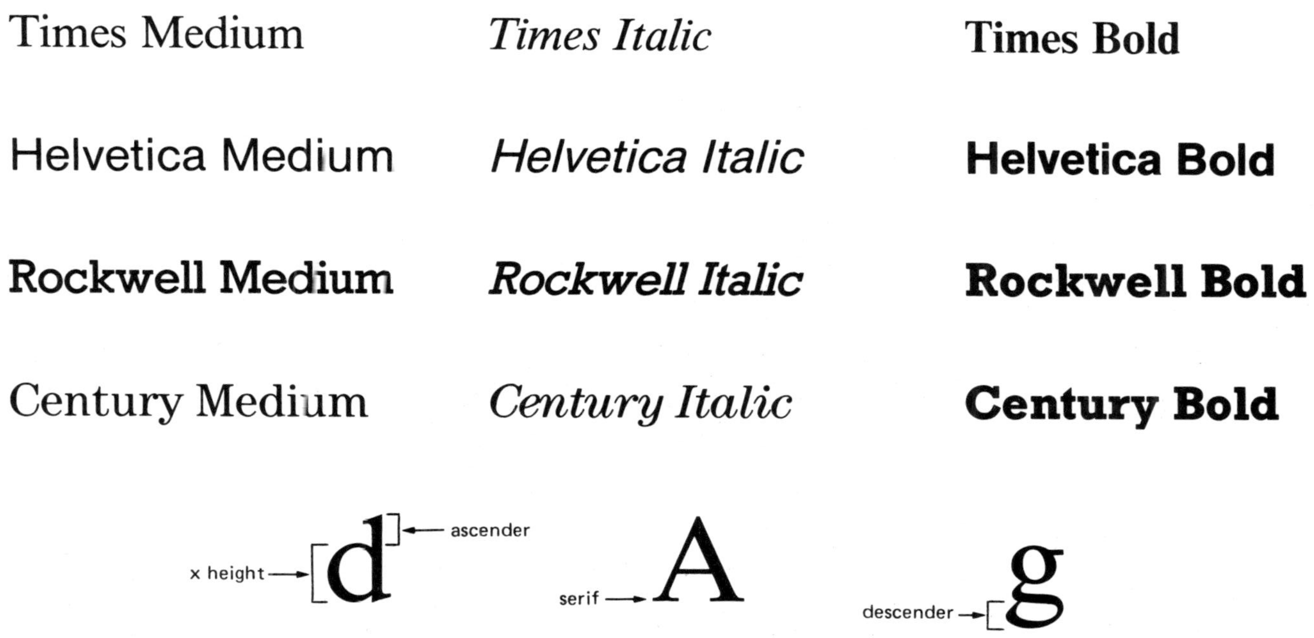

Production 51

Times Medium

Times Italic

Times Bold

Helvetica Medium

Helvetica Italic

Helvetica Bold

Rockwell Medium

Rockwell Italic

Rockwell Bold

Century Medium

Century Italic

Century Bold

x height — ascender

serif — descender

Figure 5.1. *Typefaces and letter forms*

52 Publishing Your Own Specialist Magazine

There are countless different *typefaces*, or styles of type and examples are given in Figure 5.1. They range from the commonplace like Times to the wildly exotic. Each typeface usually has different forms: medium, italic, condensed and so on. The typefaces come in a range of sizes measured on their body height (see Figure 5.1), and the space between each line of type, called *leading* (pronounced like wedding), can be varied to suit the design and to assist readability. The space between letters (*letterspacing*) can also be varied but this is mainly used on headings rather than body copy.

Typesetters have their own peculiar system of measurement to confuse the layperson, using *picas*, *ems* and *ens*. (A pica is the old name for what is now generally called 12 point. It measures nearly one-sixth of an inch. An en is half an em which is also equivalent to a pica. You can see how the old printer liked to confuse the layperson!) In fact, there are special metal type rules which designers and typesetters use to measure letter heights and line lengths etc.

Copy (handwritten or preferably typed text) delivered to a designer has to be marked up for the typesetter so that he knows what typefaces to use, their sizes, the line lengths etc. The designer has the job of making the copy fit into the space allocated and this is called *casting off*. You will find that after a while you will be able to judge fairly well whether copy is going to fit or not without learning how to cast off which requires some training and is a rather interesting combination of the aesthetic and the mathematic. All this can be done more immediately and more easily on a computer via desk-top publishing (see below).

Once the designer has marked up the copy for typesetting it goes off to be typeset and will usually come back as *galleys* which are either broken up into pages or not depending on instructions. These are provided in order to check that the typesetter has not made typing errors (*literals*) and that the correct typestyles etc have been used.

It is possible to save money and time by providing the typesetter with a disc from the editorial computer/wordprocessor (if you are using one). This would involve some close liaison with your typesetter and extra work on your part to make sure that you are absolutely satisfied with what is on your screen. You would then input a previously agreed series of codes which the typesetter's equipment can 'read' and they drive his typesetting machine to produce *bromides*, which are photographic proofs for correction and pasting down before making the final film.

All this is not difficult and is commonly done, reducing the cost of typesetting for an average, straightforward piece of A4 page setting from around £15 per page to about £5. Optical character recognition (OCR) systems are also available which 'read' typescript and transfer it straight on to disc ready for coding. Technology in this area is moving fast.

Probably the most significant technological development in this area is *desk-top publishing* (DTP). Basically, this is software which runs on hardware with a larger monitor screen than the normal computer. The software enables the operator to write, design and lay out pages on the screen. Typefaces and sizes can be chosen and tried on the screen and line rules, decorative borders etc can be selected and used to enhance your design. Another useful feature is that with the use of a scanner, photographs, illustrations and so on can be transferred from an existing printed page on to the screen and then enlarged, reduced and so on as you wish.

The potential of desk-top publishing for small publishers is immense. It gives complete control over the look of the finished page with the flexibility to make last-minute changes before producing artwork for printing. Desk-top publishing, in theory, can combine the editing, design and typesetting functions with consequent savings in time and money in the long run. However, the systems require a fairly substantial upfront investment. Desk-top publishing systems also require a certain amount of expertise and computer knowledge as well as a knowledge of typesetting and some design ability to produce professional material.

If you are contemplating running your own in-house desk-top publishing system it would be wise to consider the cost and the operating time you or your staff will have to spend. There are a number of specialist magazines being prepared on DTP and although the non-professional attempts at design sometimes show, the long-term savings can be considerable. Alternatively, there are bureaux, typesetters and printers who have DTP systems on which your magazine can be produced.

After the typesetting has been proofread and any corrections made, it goes back to the designer as bromides which is clean setting ready to paste down as artwork on a designer's artboard. At this stage photographs and illustrations are incorporated into the design.

Origination

To print your job the printer will need a set of printing plates to

54 Publishing Your Own Specialist Magazine

work from. It is these plates, usually litho plates for litho printing, which are wrapped around the rollers in the printing press. The plates have an image etched on to them by using film (sheets of either positive or negative photographic film) which is made by photographing the designer's artwork. However, photographs will probably have to be incorporated into the artwork in monotone (black and white) or colour.

In order to reproduce photographs or transparencies the platemaker will have to break the image down into dots and these will produce the *tone* – the black, grey and white shading on a monotone photograph. The easiest way to see this is to look at a newspaper photograph closely. You will see that it is made up of dots whose areas are covered to a greater or lesser extent with black. You can also look at a photograph in a book or magazine under a magnifying glass and see the same effect. The density of dots, usually measured by the number of dots per square centimetre, is called the *screen*. Your designer or platemaker will decide which screen to use and this depends on the subject and the kind of paper your magazine will eventually be printed on. Commonly used screens are 120, 133 and 150. Two examples of differing screens are shown in Figure 5.2.

Making plates for colour film is a highly technical, and nowadays, computerised process. However, in order to produce a colour image the platemaker has to make four plates. (It can be more for certain jobs and where the printer has a five- or six-colour press.) These plates will print four colours which will combine, when broken up into dots in the same way as a monotone photograph, to produce a full colour photograph. The standard basic colours are black, cyan (blue), magenta (red) and yellow.

The platemaker will enlarge your transparency to the right size and *scan* it using filters to screen out the colours, producing the four separate pieces of film required. The platemaker will then test the scanning by making proof plates and will print test sheets called *progressives*. These are then printed on a proofing press in the following colour rotation: yellow, red, blue and black. The progressives will be supplied to the printer with the plates so that he can match the colour values exactly. It goes without saying that colour origination and printing are expensive. Bear in mind that with colour origination the number of colour images or the number of scans will affect the cost of your job considerably.

It is possible to ask your printer to look after the platemaking for you, and many printers will have their own platemaking

Production 55

Figure 5.2. *Photographs using different screens (a) 65 screen (b) 133 screen*
Reproduced by kind permission of Biddles Limited

56　**Publishing Your Own Specialist Magazine**

facilities. You can, of course, buy the plates yourself and supply them to the printer. This may be cheaper (a printer will put a handling charge on the job) but you do need to have a certain level of knowledge and this approach will take up extra time.

Finishing and binding

Once your magazine comes off the printing press as flat, printed sheets, it has to be collated, gathered, folded, trimmed and bound. Depending on the number being printed the sheets will probably be folded into sections of 8 or 16 pages on a mechanised bindery line process which will then collate all the sections (or signatures) which make up the magazine, including the cover. The magazine is then stitched and trimmed ready for any inserts and packed ready for despatch. What happens next is covered in Chapter 7 on distribution but it is worth noting that many printers offer enveloping into plastic self-seal or heat-seal envelopes for onward despatch to the mailing house or to subscribers.

There are two main methods of binding used for magazines. The first is called *saddle-stitching*, which is when two or three wires, like small staples, are put through the spine of the magazine.

When the magazine has a large number of pages, say over 64, *perfect binding* is often used. By this method, the folded edge of each section is cut off and the pages are glued into the cover which is squared off at the spine. This gives a good 'bookish' feel to the magazine and enables the publisher to run title information etc down the spine. It does not, however, open as flat as the saddle-stitched magazine.

Choosing a printer

There are hundreds, if not thousands, of printers to choose from. This has its disadvantages as they vary tremendously both in what they can do and how they do it. To start with look through the *Magazine Production Handbook* which is published annually by Haymarket Press. Alternatively, look at those publications which are similar to the one you have in mind and see who printed them. Write or telephone and ask for a quotation. You will be able to tell a lot about the printer from the way he responds to your enquiry – whether he responds quickly, handles you personally and civilly etc. It is best to prepare in advance a standard specification which you can give to each printer you

Production 57

Format:	48 pages plus 4 page cover
Run:	20,000 copies
Paper:	text 100gsm Art cover 135gsm Art
Origination:	From CRC supplied (flat artwork and transparencies) 32 pages of mono including half-tones. 16 pages of colour (approx 10 scans). 4 pages colour A/W supplied. Wet proofs required for colour, ozalids for b/w.
Printing:	16 pages of colour and black and white. 32 pages mono. 4 pages colour.
Binding:	Saddle stitch 2 wires and trim. Please show separate price for inserts.
Delivery:	8 drops in and around London. Approximately 260 packets to be made up from labels supplied by distributor.

Figure 5.3. *A standard magazine specification*

approach for a quotation; at least four, if not six, quotes would be advisable. Figure 5.3 is an example of the kind of specification a printer is looking for.

Don't pretend that you know more than you do. Ask questions and make sure that you receive answers that you understand. A good printer's representative should be able to answer any technical questions and will usually make suggestions about the various ways in which a job can be tackled. Remember that if this is the first time you have dealt with the company they will also be curious, and rightly so, about the way you are funding the business, at some stage they will certainly want bank references and will probably enquire fairly deeply into your finances. Too many printers have fared badly at the hands of enthusiastic but underfinanced entrepreneurs.

Make sure that the quotation is broken down sufficiently showing the cost of paper, plates and so on and that it also gives you run-on prices in case you decide to increase the number of copies you require as well as prices for extra sections and colour pages.

Remember, too, to discuss the timing of your payments to the printer; you will want to assist your cash flow by obtaining as much credit as you can. You should, if the printer has confidence

58 Publishing Your Own Specialist Magazine

Bloggs Printers Ltd

Estimate for printing magazine X

Frequency: Monthly
Size: A4, 297 × 210mm
Extent: 48 page + 4pp cover
Origination: Final page film supplied
Process: Heat set web offset   cover sheet fed litho

Plate Print and Fold

	20,000 copies	1000 run on
16pp mono	£536	£11.75
16pp 4 col/mono	£769	£11.83
8pp mono	£321	£7.85
8pp 4 col/mono	£432	£7.79
8pp 4 col	£543	£37.85
4pp 4 col cover	£552	£11.75
Saddle-stitch and trim		
3 sections plus cover	£272	£11.46
4–7 sections plus cover	£293	£14.32
Perfect bind and trim		
4 sections plus cover	£666	£30.07
up to 8 sections plus cover	£724	£32.94

		20,000 copies	1000 run on
Supplying paper			
Text 115gsm art paper	16pp	£1407	£58.63
	8pp	£714	£29.70
Cover 135gsm art paper	4pp	£380	£18.95

Loose inserts   £3.75 per 1000

Plastic wrap with your
labels for cheshiring*   £28 per 1000

This is useful information for working out your price. Let us see how a price for a 48-page magazine plus four-page cover would be arrived at using this estimate.

	20,000 copies	1000 run-on
1 × 4pp cover in 4 colours	£552	£11.75
2 × 16pp text 4/1 (this means four colours on one side of the sheet and one on the other)	£1538	£23.66
1 × 16 page sheet 1/1 (mono on both sides of the sheet)	£536	£11.75
Saddle-stitch and trim 3 sections (3 × 16s) plus cover	£272	£11.46
Supplying paper		
3 × 16pp 115gsm art paper	£4221	£175.90
1 × 4pp 135gsm art paper	£380	£18.95
	£7499	£253.46

* Cheshire machines are commonly used in mailing houses. They are specifically designed to cut up and stick sheets of labels on to envelopes.

Figure 5.4. *An estimate for the specification shown in Figure 5.3*

Production   59

in you, be able to organise a 60-day, or even a 90-day, credit period rather than the usual 30-day one, so go for as much as you can. Some printers, particularly those who produce a number of magazines, will have standard prices to enable publishers to work out costs for a wide variety of extents (numbers of pages), quantity and content. Examples of this kind of quotation are shown in Figure 5.4.

Along with the quotation you will have to agree upon a schedule. You will need to give the printer final dates for receipt of bound copies and then he will work back from these to produce a deadline for supplying him with camera-ready copy, film or printers' plates. Then you will need to draw up a time schedule like the one shown in Figure 5.5.

Editorial manuscripts to typesetter	2/3/90	4/5/90	6/7/90	31/8/90
Galleys to editorial	16/3/90	18/5/90	20/7/90	14/9/90
Corrected and returned to typesetter	20/3/90	24/5/90	26/7/90	20/9/90
Clean, corrected galleys to designer	26/3/90	28/5/90	30/7/90	24/9/90
Advertisement copy and prelims to be sent to typesetter	6/4/90	8/6/90	10/8/90	5/10/90
Typesetter sets ads for despatch to client for approval and prelims to editorial	10/4/90	12/6/90	15/8/90	10/10/90
All final copy to designer	12/4/90	15/6/90	17/8/90	16/10/90
CRC (camera-ready copy) plus transparencies for colour and black and whites to platemaker	20/4/90	25/6/90	27/8/90	22/10/90
Colour proofs and bromides to editorial for checking and colour correction	26/4/90	29/6/90	29/6/90	26/10/90
Plates to printer	4/5/90	6/7/90	7/9/90	2/11/90
Bound copies to distributor	18/5/90	20/7/90	21/9/90	16/11/90

Figure 5.5. *Production schedule for a bi-monthly magazine*

60   **Publishing Your Own Specialist Magazine**

Figure 5.5 is an actual schedule used for a bi-monthly magazine and you can see that although the timetable is comparatively leisurely compared to a monthly magazine, the dates still come thick and fast. There are always two issues in production at any one time and the editor may be working on at least four issues at various stages of processing.

The bound copy date to the distributor, if your magazine is heading for newsagent sales, is an important date and it is essential for your credibility with the distributor, the retailer and your readers that you meet it every time.

Once you are satisfied that you have chosen the right printer some general principles apply. Your printer is someone on whom you are going to have to rely when you are faced with difficult situations and missed deadlines, particularly if you are producing a monthly magazine. Whatever the size of the company, make sure that you meet not only the representative but the person who looks after the scheduling of the work and the progress-chasing. In a small company it may be the managing director; in a larger company it will be the works manager or production manager. Whoever it is, make sure that he is on your side and is capable of helping you in an emergency.

Go to see the factory (be suspicious if you are put off), meet as many people as you can, see how clean the workspaces are, and get a feel of the general attitude of the staff, particularly the machine-minders. Find out about their existing customers and ask to see samples of similar work produced. Take this opportunity to go through the agreed schedule to make sure that there are no doubts about who does what and when.

Whatever the frequency of your magazine, you will find that deadlines come around all too quickly and the ones on the schedule you have fixed are very important. In fact, these dates are vital; prompt and regular appearance is essential to the credibility of any periodical and it is demanded by the distribution system as well as, of course, your readers.

Chapter 6
Advertising

Some magazines rely on advertising for the vast majority of their income. Indeed, for many magazines it is the sole reason for their existence and the editorial content is minimal and in some cases (*Exchange & Mart,* for example) non-existent. Very few magazines carry no advertising and even if you propose to publish a church newsletter or a scientific periodical a little advertising both brings in an income and also adds credibility for the reader.

When planning your magazine you will have established the economic importance of advertising to your venture. If you have plans for a magazine that will be purchased by the reader, by subscription or from newsagents, you will need at the outset to establish the number of pages of advertising you must fill to reach your financial targets. You will also, of course, have to fix appropriate advertising rates.

Advertising rates

Your rates will have to be fixed with the following considerations in mind:

1. Your proposed circulation.
2. The advertising rates of your competitors (if you have any) or magazines of a similar nature.
3. The cost of printing your magazine.
4. Your potential advertisers and the amounts they are likely to pay for their advertisements given your readership.
5. The relationship between the cost of your full-page and smaller sized advertisements. If you are going to attract a number of smaller advertisements, there is some sense in making them more expensive than the pro rata cost of larger spaces. This might encourage advertisers to 'trade up' to the next larger size of advertisement.

Don't ignore the prospect of selling classified advertising space, particularly if you have a specialist magazine. Classified advertisements are usually sold by word or line of type and paid for in

62 Publishing Your Own Specialist Magazine

advance by the advertiser who is often a private individual rather than a trader. This can be a very useful source of revenue, but needs a little attention.

Make it easy for your readers to supply their advertisements by giving them a coupon to fill in (with boxes for their advertisement copy - which also induces them to write clearly). Make sure that the advertisements are pre-paid and that readers are able to pay by credit card if they wish.

Classified ads can also add substantially to the reader interest in your magazine. You would be surprised at the number of magazines with substantial editorial content which are bought principally for the advertisements, particularly the small ads.

It might be useful to look through *British Rate and Data* published monthly by Maclean Hunter Ltd, which contains listings of most commercially published magazines and their advertising rates. The entries are free and *BRAD*, as it is known, is subscribed to by a wide range of advertisers. Figure 6.1 is a typical entry from its listings showing the kind of information advertisers need to see.

If advertising is going to be important to the viability of your magazine you will need to produce a more extensive version of Figure 6.1, known as a rate card, to send out to advertisers. The example in Figure 6.2 is fairly typical.

MILITARY ILLUSTRATED—PAST AND PRESENT

Military Illustrated Ltd, 5 Gerrard Street, London W1V 7LJ. 01-287 4570. Alt months—June/July, etc, week preceding cover date. Copy—6 weeks preceding cover date. Cancellation—8 weeks preceding cover date. Single copy £2.50. Per year £16 (UK), $40 elsewhere

Agency Commission 10%

Rate card received February 1989 (excl. VAT)

Standard Rates	1	3	6
dps	£800.00	£720.00	£648.00
page	£400.00	£360.00	£324.00
half	£220.00	£196.00	£184.00
quarter	£135.00	£120.00	£112.00
eighth	£84.00	£75.00	£70.00

Cover Rates Inside front cover mono £480, series 3—£446 6—£415. Full colour £960, series 3—£855 6—£795

Colour Rates Full colour, dps £1400, series 3—£1260 6—£1175. Page £800, series 3—£715 6—£665. Half £450, series 3—£410 6—£390

Bleed Pages 10% extra

Inserts Accepted by arrangement

Classified Rates Wordage 35p (min 15 words), scc £7

Mechanical Data Type page size 267 x 190, half 267 x 93 or 130 x 190, quarter 130 x 93, eighth 63 x 93. No of cols 4. Screen: mono 48, colour 54. Offset

Executives Editor, Martin Windrow. Advertisement Manager, Valerie Scott (0730-63976)

Circulation Uncertified

RES available

Figure 6.1. *A sample listing from* BRAD

Reproduced by kind permission of Maclean Hunter Limited.

RATES & DATA

Size	MONOCHROME Number of Insertions (£)			FULL COLOUR Number of Insertions (£)			TYPE AREA Depth mm × Width mm
	1	3	6	1	3	6	
Double Page Spread	800	720	648	1400	1260	1175	267 × 380
Whole Page	400	360	324	800	715	665	267 × 190
Inside Front Cover	480	446	415	960	855	795	267 × 190
Half Page Horizontal	220	196	184	450	410	390	130 × 190
Half Page Vertical	220	196	184	450	410	390	267 × 93
Quarter Page	135	120	112				130 × 93
Eighth Page	84	75	70				63 × 93

CLASSIFIED ADVERTISEMENTS	All private classified advertisements	35p per word (minimum £5.25 – 15 words)
	Semi-display advertisements	£7.00 per single column centimetre
	– All Classified Advertisements must be pre-paid	

All Rates Quoted Are Exclusive of VAT

Inserts accepted by arrangement   10% Discount for pre-payment   Agency Discount 15%

MECHANICAL DATA

Finished Size A4. Printed sheet fed litho
Screen: (Mono) 120 line screen (Colour) 133 line screen
Camera Ready Artwork or Film Positives
Trimmed Size 297mm × 210mm Bleed Size 303mm × 216mm DPS 297mm × 420mm
No essential matter to appear within 12mm of any trimmed edge. Typesetting, Photography, Artwork and Colour Separations, where necessary, will be charged extra at cost; rates quoted above are for insertion only. Proofs will be supplied only upon specific request, for correction and return within 48 hours of receipt.

PUBLICATION AND COPY DATES

Bi-monthly	June/July	December/January
	August/September	February/March
	October/November	April/May

Each issue on sale last week of preceding month. Copy for typesetting required seven weeks before publication. Artwork required five weeks before publication.

Figure 6.2. A sample rate card

64 Publishing Your Own Specialist Magazine

Notice that discounts are given for bookings of series of ads and that standard discounts for agencies are quoted. The benefits to you of obtaining a run or series of advertisements are obvious; apart from having the security of knowing that spaces are already allocated in advance, you do, of course, save money in terms of time, telephone bills and so on by not having to look for a proportion of advertisement sales for each issue. You may also want to consider offering a reduced payment for pre-paid or early paid advertisements.

You will notice that the rates for inserts are given 'on application'. Inserts are a form of advertising often highly favoured by advertisers for certain kinds of selling, particularly when selling products 'off the page'. The problem about quoting rates for inserts is that they can vary enormously from an A5 single sheet to a 16-page catalogue. It is important to establish how much your printer is going to charge to put inserts into the magazine before establishing a rate for these. He will probably charge you more for the catalogue than the single sheet. The other, perhaps more important, consideration is the possible increase in the postage cost of a heavy item which may push you over a postage step. For these reasons it is probably best not to quote a specific price unless you give a price for a single-sheet insert to give some idea of your charges. The relationship of the cost of advertising inserts to page rates varies widely.

It is helpful for advertisers to have some kind of analysis of your readership. This may be difficult for a new magazine or one which has yet to be published. However, once published it is possible to insert a questionnaire in your magazine or mail your subscriber list. There are a number of market research companies who can assist in producing such a questionnaire and, more importantly, analysing the responses. General questions, apart from those specific to your market, should try to establish the sex, age and socio-economic status of your reader. Your advertiser will also be interested in how your copies are sold, what percentage sell overseas, if any, what percentage are subscribers and so on. When you can prepare these details it is a good idea to put them together with your rate card information to form a 'media pack' which is what a sophisticated advertiser will ask for when reviewing your publication.

Of course, many of your advertisers will not require such sophisticated information and may simply base their buying decision on their personal perception of the magazine. But it is essential to have some hard facts to quote to advertisers on the nature of your readership to prove the value of your magazine.

Unless you have a magazine which is achieving very high sales the prospects of getting a slice of the huge amounts of money spent on consumer advertising usually handled by advertising agencies are, it has to be said, remote. Every newly fledged publisher looking avariciously at the ads in colour supplements thinks, 'My readers drink, smoke, drive cars etc . . . why shouldn't I get some of this advertising?' The reason is that space-buying in all large agencies is a highly sophisticated business. Although numbers are not the be-all and end-all, the agency handling consumer products like alcohol and cigarettes will be looking for a reasonable cost per thousand (page rate divided by circulation) and a high OTS (opportunities to see). Other considerations concerning the quality of your readership and market share come into play and if your circulation is over 30,000 you may not rule it out altogether. In any case, it is worthwhile making your advertising sales material as professional and impressively 'fact full' as possible.

Who will sell your space?

The best qualified person is probably you, even if you have never sold space in your life. Two of the most important qualities are motivation and persistence and you are likely to put more enthusiasm into selling space than anyone else. However, you will probably not have the time to spend on the many telephone conversations and presentations needed to get things going. What are the alternatives?

If your projections and prospects for advertising are high and you can afford to employ a space salesperson from the start then go for the most experienced person you can afford. If you are operating in a particular market sector it may be that you have been 'sold to' by an individual working on a competitive magazine. If you can find someone who already has the contacts you need and knows your market then he or she will be worth more to you. Your own economics will dictate pay but you must build in incentives for effort and achievement tied to targets. Selling space is tough on the ego, and resilience to rejection and the will to get that next ad can be vastly strengthened by the prospect of more money.

If you can't afford to employ someone full-time, and for the majority of small to medium-sized magazines this is the case, then a freelance commission-paid agent is probably the best alternative. There are a number of advertising agents who will, for a percentage of the sales, sell your space for you. They vary

66   Publishing Your Own Specialist Magazine

from one-man companies with a few titles to cover to large agents selling space on a wide variety of magazines. The discounts they look for vary from a base of around 20 to over 50 per cent and so will their approach to selling your magazine. Unless you are fortunate, it is unlikely that you will get the same 'get that last ad' attitude to selling that you would if it was directly under your control. Too often, unknown to you, the agent sets an internal target which makes the profit he needs, after which he stops selling.

There is also the problem that the way the agent sells space on your magazine may not be the way you would wish. On the other hand, it is unlikely that the agency will take your magazine on unless the prospects for selling space are good. You can, of course, keep a designated number of accounts as 'house accounts' which you handle, and this may be a more satisfactory way of dealing with advertising customers who are well-disposed regulars.

If you decide to sell the advertising yourself or hire someone to do it in-house, it is important to remember to keep records. Have a card system for each advertiser on which you record all relevant details - name, address, telephone number and so on. On the same record make a note of the date of each approach to that person. If you can, note briefly what is said and, if the answer is not an outright 'No', make a note to telephone after a period of time. If you send specimen copies or a rate card etc, follow this up with a courteous telephone call to make sure that the information was received; press politely for a reaction and make a note of the date.

Always keep full records on each client or potential client and be persistent without being a nuisance. You may have the greatest product since sliced bread for an advertiser you have identified. However, you will usually have to make more than one contact to make the sale and it is only too easy to forget what you said, and to whom, unless you keep meticulous records.

Whoever sells the space will be confronted with the problem of selling issue no 1. This is a very important hurdle and requires as much planning as possible. You will need to start selling some months before your launch issue and so it will be necessary to produce a dummy and some cover roughs. (This will also be useful when explaining your concept to an advertising agent if that is the route you have chosen.) Your printer will make you up a white (blank) dummy of the magazine on the correct paper stock. You or your designer can prepare dummy material for the first half dozen spreads and a cover (in fact, it is a good idea to

Advertising   67

dummy three or four covers if you can). This can be done simply by cutting and pasting prints and copy into your dummy although if you need to make a number of copies to mail out you are going to be involved in some printing or copying.

A number of points need to be borne in mind when presenting your magazine to a prospective advertiser.

1. Outline the background to the magazine and, if relevant, your credentials and those of anyone else who is working with you.
2. Explain the editorial approach and the readership you are going for and how your magazine will deliver more/ cheaper/higher responding readers of their advertisements.
3. Be realistic about your eventual sales figures and push the advantage of their coming in on your high initial print run and the promotion and publicity you are going to hang on it (if this is the case).
4. Make a deal with a discount off the rate card to get advertisers in to the first issue but treat this with caution – it is too easy to seem desperate. Better to have a uniform discount for everyone on the first issue.
5. Identify those advertisers who are likely to make an impression on others in their market area and make a concerted effort to get them into your first issue.

   It has been known for new magazines to give away advertising to make the first issue look good and to encourage other advertisers. Beware of the dangers of this – people talk!

If your publication depends on advertising as an important part of its financial make-up you must be sure that your plans for obtaining advertising revenue are conservative during the first year at least. It takes time for a publication to establish itself and advertisers are wary of spending lean advertising budgets on unproven media. Getting an impressive first issue is important but *don't* expect your second and third issues to maintain the same impact – time and persistence will be needed.

Advertising production

Getting the advertisement booking is only half the battle – you still have to get the advertisement in and be paid for it. Make sure that you have a good system for chasing advertisement copy and artwork; advertisers often need reminding about copy dates. It is

68   **Publishing Your Own Specialist Magazine**

good practice to have a booking form which is signed by the advertiser. It states the terms of business and gives the copy and artwork dates.

Some advertisers are not set up to provide finished artwork and typesetting. It is common for such people, particularly those who advertise in specialist magazines, to send in typewritten (or even handwritten!) copy with a 'back of an envelope' sketch of how they want it to appear. This will involve extra typesetting and design which you will have to charge to the advertiser. You should try to find out what your competitors' policy is as far as this is concerned. Where there is a high incidence of this kind of advertising it may be better to anticipate the cost in your rates and give a discount for finished artwork. You will also have to make sure that it is clear that for four-colour advertisements the cost of making film, which can run into several hundred pounds, will be charged extra.

Whether you have an agent or the advertising is being sold from your office, someone must be delegated to make sure that adverts are planned in at the make-up stage, when the editor is finally planning that particular issue in detail. Be sure to take into account any specific requests the advertiser might make, and that the same person is responsible for making sure that all advertising copy is received on time. Often magazines send a reminder card a week or two before the advertisement is actually due. As you will see from the specimen rate card shown on page 63, the dates for receipt of copy are set earlier than the dates for artwork. This is to allow for the typesetting and design to take place and proofs to be sent to and approved by the advertiser. Make sure that such proofs are either stamped or accompanied by a note to the effect that 'unless these proofs are received corrected by (date) they will be printed as shown'.

Lastly, make sure you are paid on time. Advertisers in specialist periodicals have a relatively high bad debt level. Offer discounts for pre-payment or early payment and make sure that your invoice is sent to the advertiser with a voucher copy (a complimentary copy of the magazine to prove publication) and that the invoice is stapled or clipped to the outside of it. It is all too easy to miss an invoice tucked inside a magazine.

Chapter 7
Distribution

Getting your distribution right is as important as getting the right product. It is essential that distribution, that is, putting your product into your readers hands as quickly and cost-effectively as possible, is thought about and planned as far ahead as possible. First, we shall consider the two major forms of magazine distribution – subscription sales and newsagent sales.

Subscription sales

These are sales of copies to customers – individuals, companies or institutions – which are paid for in advance, for a given period (usually a year) and copies are delivered to them by post. There are a number of advantages for the publisher in having subscribers. Perhaps the most obvious is that the subscription is paid in advance and a magazine with a large number of subscribers will experience very satisfactory surges of income when subscriptions are renewed. Depending on the financial state of the company concerned, this is money which can go on deposit and earn interest. Commonly, learned, technical and academic journals are solely subscription based and benefit from receiving much of their income direct from their customers.

Many buyers of large quantities of magazines and journals (universities and libraries, for example) buy their subscriptions through subscription agencies. These agencies operate all over the world and ask for relatively small discounts, usually 10-15 per cent from the publisher. If you have a magazine which could be purchased by this kind of customer, it is important to mail all the agencies with details of the following year's subscription rates before you publish and every year, usually in the autumn, before they prepare their annual catalogues. Many of the large agencies will have thousands of customers so your title will receive worthwhile exposure when they promote it. It is likely that you will want to build your own list of subscribers and we look at ways you can do this in Chapter 2 on marketing and direct mail.

Subscribers can form an extremely strong financial base for a

70   Publishing Your Own Specialist Magazine

magazine and it is worth spending time finding them and then making sure that they are looked after. You have, after all, persuaded them to part with a sum of money in order to receive a magazine on a particular subject. They are committed readers and of course prime prospects for other material you produce in the same area. They are your core audience and apart from anything else a responsive sounding board to any planned changes and developments. Mail them, send them a questionnaire occasionally - you will find they are high percentage responders. You can also make them offers of associated products from time to time.

Think hard about selling or renting your subscriber list to anyone else - you will be asked to do this sometimes if your magazine is in any way successful. Treat your subscribers like members of an exclusive club.

As soon as your magazine comes off the presses, make sure that subscribers' copies are sent out as soon as possible. Apart from any price advantage you can offer them on their subscription (and although advisable, the economics do not always make it possible) they will want to receive their copies first, certainly before they see them appearing on the news-stands if you are selling this way as well. Sometimes your printer will be able to offer you the service of despatching the subscription copies or alternatively, they can be sent out through one of the specialised companies that look after the despatch of subscriptions or a mailing house. If your list is small, you could do this yourself, but make sure that you have the time and the room - 1000 A4 magazines, for example, take up about as much floor space as a small car.

The advantage of using a magazine subscription handling agency is that they will be able to produce computerised reports every month which will enable you to fine-tune your subscription process. They will also be able to manage the business of sending out renewal notices (letters informing subscribers that their subscriptions have lapsed and encouraging them to renew) with a degree of sophistication. Whoever does the job of sending out the copies will have to have a list of labels for your subscribers. If your subscriber list is small then this could be done in your office. It is really a job for a computer, and there are a number of software programs which will look after address handling in a very sophisticated way.

Remember, however, that dealing with subscriptions means that the subscriber will have to be input and coded according to the length of his or her subscription. You will need to know when

Distribution 71

THE FIELD

5 Riverpark Estate, Billet Lane, Berkhamsted, Herts HP4 1HL. Telephone: 0442 876661

Dear Subscriber

Your subscription to The Field expires with the .... issue. We hope that you have enjoyed reading our magazine for the past year and that you have appreciated the convenience of having it sent direct to you every month.

The cover price is now £1.80 and for the full UK subscription price of £25 you will receive the 12 regular monthly issues, with various supplements, plus the Winter and Summer special issues. These raise the full value of your subscription to £26.60. It includes postage and packing. If you wish to renew your subscription, please fill in the form below and return it to us in the FREEPOST envelope provided.

SUBSCRIPTION RENEWAL FORM

INSTRUCTIONS TO YOUR BANK TO PAY DIRECT DEBITS
Please complete Parts 1 to 4 to instruct your bank to make payments directly from your account and return this form in the envelope provided.

1. To The Manager .... Bank

....
(Address of your Bank)

I wish to renew my annual Subscription to The Field at a cost of £25 (1year), £42 (2 years), £54 (3years) payable by cheque or credit card. Equivalent overseas rates are £40, £72 and £99. I understand The Field will pay delivery charges and that I will receive the Winter and Summer Special issues free of charge. Direct Debit is provided for one year U.K. subscribers only. Air mail rates are available on request.

Originator's Identification Number   9 2 2 6 2 6

Field Subscription Reference
(Office use only)
2. Name of Account Holder

3. Account Number
(Banks may refuse to accept instructions to pay direct debits from some types of accounts)

Sort code

4. Your instructions to the bank:

I wish to take out an additional gift subscription for:

Name: ....

Address: ....

....

.... Postcode: ....

I enclose an additional payment of £25/£42/£54 (£40/£72/£99 overseas)

Please indicate your method of payment:

☐ I wish to pay £25 by Direct Debit. I have completed the form below.

☐ I enclose a cheque for £25/£42/£54 (£40/£72/£99 overseas) (delete as appropriate) made payable to The Field.

☐ Please debit my credit card account with £25/£42/£54 (£40/£72/£99) (delete as appropriate).

☐ Access   ☐ Visa

Card Expiry Date

Card number

Signature ....

- I instruct you to pay direct debits from my account at the request of Burlington Publishing Co. Ltd. in respect of my Subscription Advice.
- The amounts are variable and may be debited on various dates.
- I understand that Burlington Publishing Co. Ltd. may change amounts and dates only after giving me prior notice.
- I will inform the bank in writing if I wish to cancel this instruction.
- I understand that if any direct debit is paid which breaks the terms of this instruction, the bank will make a refund.

Signature(s) .... Date ....

THE FIELD ASSURES YOU THAT:
- The Instruction will only be used for the collection of your subscription to The Field of £25 p.a.
- No amount will be collected before it is due.
- You can cancel the Instruction by notifying your bank in writing and advising The Field.
- If any direct debit is paid which breaks the terms of this Instruction your bank will make a refund.

Figure 7.1. *Example of a subscription renewal form*

Reproduced by kind permission of Burlington Publishing Company Limited.

72 Publishing Your Own Specialist Magazine

each individual subscription ends in order to send out reminders. In fact, three reminders are often sent: one with the penultimate issue, one with the last issue and one on its own. Figure 7.1 is an example of such reminders. The labels will need to be produced in sorted order according to the size of the list and the requirements of the mailing house.

It may be worth noting that the Post Office has introduced a new magazine distribution service for the UK which can provide good discounts for magazine subscriber mailings. Two important qualifications are that the minimum for any one posting is over 1000 packets and that the posting is pre-sorted according to a sortation plan provided by the Post Office. Full details can be obtained from MAILSORT, Headquarters Building, 33 Grosvenor Place, London SW1X 1PX.

If you have overseas subscribers and the arrival of your magazine is not too time-critical, it is worthwhile obtaining a Reduced Rate Postage licence which will enable your envelope to be sent by Accelerated Surface Post or Bulk Accelerated Mail. This too will give you substantial postage discounts over air mail but the magazine will arrive far quicker than by surface mail which can take weeks or even months. Apply to your local area Post Office for information. There are also consolidated shippers who can provide extremely competitive rates for overseas posting, particularly to the USA.

There are a number of ways to envelope the subscribers' magazines. By far the cheapest is the plastic-wrapped enclosure which comes in various gauges of plastic film and can be printed with an opaque ink which can carry a message and the label; the envelope can include a carrying card which can take the address label. These have the advantage of being light and therefore cheaper to post, and many printers and mailing houses have a plastic wrap system as part of their production line so it is a relatively fast and inexpensive process. There was a vogue some years ago, particularly with controlled circulation magazines, for wrapping a rolled magazine. If you have ever tried to read a magazine that has been tightly rolled you will understand why this is not advisable.

Standard manilla or white envelopes are more expensive and heavier than plastic but they have the advantage of giving slightly greater protection to the product and lending it an air of value. If you decide on this type of envelope you will probably benefit from the mailing house buying them for you. The mailing house will probably be a large user of envelopes and will receive big discounts from the supplier.

Subscriptions can be the most important factor in a magazine's financial make-up or totally irrelevant – some magazines don't offer subscriptions. The table below shows a list of well-known and not so well-known magazines and their total sales against subscriptions.

Total sales and subscriptions (1989 figures)

	Total sales	Subscriptions
SAGA Magazine	641,457	69,368
Classic and Sportscar	103,534	3,389
Scouting	36,491	5,526
Architectural Review	20,824	12,363
Cycling Weekly	33,710	808
Puzzle Monthly	58,089	741

Newsagent sales

There are 36,000 retail newsagents in this country – more if you include supermarkets and garages – and the majority of all magazines are sold through these outlets. The relationship between subscription sales and newsagent sales for some general and specialist magazines is shown above. The way to get your magazine sold, if it is suitable to this huge market-place, is normally through a national magazine distributor. The system for magazine distribution is complicated, but basically your national distributor will sell to wholesalers such as Surridge Dawson, WH Smith and Menzies (the last two are also retailers, of course) and a large number of smaller wholesalers.

These wholesalers then sell to a wide range of CTNs (confectioners, tobacconists and newsagents) in their regional area. As you can see, there are a number of people taking nibbles at the financial cake of your magazine, and it is an unfortunate fact of life that you will be giving away a large discount to your chosen distributor. Fifty per cent or more is not unusual, I'm afraid. However, perhaps the most problematical area of selling in this way is that, especially with a new magazine, the copies that are distributed will be on a *sale or return* basis.

The following are some of the ways to set up national distribution if you are using the accepted channels (and the alternatives are few) for a new magazine. Talk to two or three distributors about your new project. They will tell you fairly quickly if they think your title has a chance of selling through

74 Publishing Your Own Specialist Magazine

national newsagent outlets. Although WH Smith and Menzies will be unlikely to buy from you direct, you might also want to talk to them. Both organisations are extremely helpful and will give objective views on the likely success of your magazine in their stores.

Once all this is done your distributors will then give you their views on the likely sales take-up and this will give you, the potential publisher, some figures on which to begin basing your print runs. It will be helpful for distributors to see a dummy and some idea of the contents of the magazine with sample spreads and so on. When the time comes (about three months before publication of the first issue) they will disseminate information to their representatives who will begin talking to and taking orders from wholesalers around the country. A sales picture builds up and at the agreed time the distributor will give the publisher a print quantity. This, of course, should be in sufficient time for your printer to order paper and so on.

The distributor will also set an 'on sale' date which is when the magazine is timed to be on sale all over the country. The distributor will have a sophisticated system of road or rail transport (using British Rail's MAGSTAR rail delivery if rail is the chosen method) and it is important that your printer meets the date given for delivery to meet this on sale date.

Your printer will be supplied by the distributor with a delivery schedule and a batch of labels, destinations to which magazines in various quantities will have to be packed and then sent to a delivery point.

Now the fun starts. The magazine goes on sale; it sells or it doesn't and the retailer, after the on sale month, returns unsold copies to the wholesaler and eventually to the distributor. The distributor then notifies the publisher. In practice this process can take two to three months, sometimes a little more. This means that the publisher has to wait at least two months before knowing how the publication has performed and by that time will need to be working, editorially if nothing else, on the fourth or even fifth issue.

So it could take that long to find out that the magazine has been a disaster, by which time a great deal of money will have been spent. One other point to bear in mind is that although called sale or return, the system is sale or destroy. The magazines are never returned to the publisher and are destroyed to prevent them finding their way on to any 'illegal' market stalls and suchlike. Frightening, isn't it?

Magazine and newspaper distribution is changing with the

advent of computerisation and with the impact that the new attitudes to staffing and unions in the revolutionised newspaper industry have created. There is a diminishing choice of distributors to go to and those who remain are carrying more titles. The major players, which include such companies as Comag, AGB Impress, Seymour, are all providing similar services with a highly sophisticated system, teams of representatives (although sometimes quite small) and computerised feedback on sales. However, your title will be one of many and it will be up to you to keep them on their toes.

When your magazine goes on sale check the station bookstalls and the bigger newsagents. Let your contact at the distribution company know that you are interested in the visibility of your magazine and that you will get out of your office and check that the magazine you have worked so hard to put together that month is prominently displayed. You'll do it in a civilised way, of course. Take your contact at the distribution company out to lunch to get him on your side – good personal contacts are essential. But be a nuisance if you have to.

Choosing a distributor to handle your title if you go for one of the bigger distributors (if they will have you!) is fairly straightforward. They all seem to offer the same kind of service although their terms of trading differ slightly and you may find a useful 1 or 2 per cent on your side if you shop around. Check the magazines each one carries to see whether there are any similar titles or ones of which the sales people of the distributor concerned will have market experience which could help you. There are smaller specialist distributors as well who might be worth approaching.

You could, of course, consider doing the whole thing yourself thereby saving the 50 per cent discount, but you will have to deal with the various wholesalers, look after invoicing and the fairly complicated despatch problems after giving a discount to the wholesaler. This only really makes sense if you have a number of magazines and the costs can be amortised over them.

From many individual publishers' points of view the distribution system can seem very unsatisfactory. Even though computerisation has brought a useful flow of statistics and information to bear, a great deal still depends on people and the fact that there are an overwhelming number of titles. There is no good system to cope with the situation where a retailer receives his, let's say, ten copies of a magazine and they sell out within a week. In theory the retailer should reorder from his wholesaler, but this rarely, if ever, happens. Worse still, he may be unaware that this

76   **Publishing Your Own Specialist Magazine**

particular magazine has sold fast and so does not increase his order next month. It may take some time for the busy retailer to wake up to this situation.

Some of the bigger newsagent chains of shops have more sophisticated systems and can be adapted to changes in sale rates rather more quickly than the small-town newsagent. Many of the bigger chains are also bringing in EPOS (Electronic Point of Sale) for magazines as they have with books which will enable them to monitor sales much more closely. This system works off the bar code (there is an example on the back cover of this book) which is recorded at the cash desk and the computer stock figure is then adjusted so that a daily, weekly etc figure can be established for any title. This information is then used when ordering. Very soon all magazines which intend to have a national sale will have to carry a bar code on each issue. If you are putting your magazine on national newsagents' shelves, it is important that you investigate bar coding. There are a number of companies who will provide a bar code for each issue of your magazine and the cost is relatively small. Bar codes are provided as a small piece of film which you send off with the artwork for the cover.

Other distribution

Apart from these two methods of sale which tend to be the principal ones for most magazines you can always try to find sales in outlets which have a relevance to your readership. For example, it may be possible on a magazine dealing with, say, antiques to set up a distribution to antique dealers and shops by mailing them and supplying orders yourself or by finding someone else who already calls on these outlets and offering them a percentage on sales to handle your product.

Overseas distribution

Consider carefully whether your projected title would have any relevance overseas. There is a big English-speaking market out there which includes, for the right titles, some European countries. Newsagent distribution can be obtained in Australia, Canada and South Africa through companies like Gordon and Gotch who have associated companies there.

Even if your publication will travel and would be of interest in these countries we are not talking about great quantities in most cases. You will probably be offered a small quantity distribution at a high 50-55 per cent discount for a firm sale or a slightly larger one at a lower discount to the distributor – 40–45 per cent on a sale or return basis. It's your choice but remember you can always move the sale or return arrangement to firm sale once a sales pattern has been established. It is possible in these countries to limit your commitment on a sale or return basis to a sensible number so that if sales are poor you do not lose too much. Unfortunately, this is not the case in the United States. The US system, although similar in some ways to that in the UK, is much bigger in size and in the number of magazines handled. A national US distributor would be dealing with a minimum of 50,000 copies sale or return for news-stand sales which is a sizeable cost to gamble with.

Using a fulfilment or mailing house
Depending on the kind of magazine you are producing you may need to consider the sale of back numbers. This can be a lucrative form of continuing sales but remember that however many you decide to keep back for continuing sales, they have to be stored and the transaction is not high value unless you have a very high cover price. If you decide to sell binders in which readers can store their copies or other associated magazine products, storage, together with a competent despatch system, is essential. Unless you take this on from your own office, you will probably want to find a fulfilment or mailing house to look after it for you. This might also be a possibility when considering how to handle your subscribers as most such companies will have a computerised address-handling system. There is a distinct advantage in having all your dealings with the public looked after in one place. Time-consuming telephone calls with individuals about small orders and particular problems that inevitably arise, although all part of the business, are often best left to people who are geared to handling them.

Glossary

ABC The Audit Bureau of Circulation, an official body set up to monitor the circulation statements of magazines for the benefit of advertisers.

Bar code A symbol, unique to each publication, which can be read by computer by means of a light pen passed across it. It enables retailers to maintain accurate stock and sales figures – see EPOS.

Bleed A term describing print which runs to the edge of the paper without having a border.

Body copy The main text of any piece excluding headlines etc.

Bound copy date The date by which copies of a publication have to be ready for distribution.

Bromide A photographic copy of film on to art paper which can be corrected or pasted down as artwork.

Camera-ready copy (CRC) Finished artwork with type etc pasted down and photographs and transparencies marked up for size, colours indicated and so on. The artwork will go to the platemaker for proofs and final film before the plates are made.

Cast off Describes the business of accurately estimating how many words of text will fit, in a chosen style and size of typeface, into a given page extent, or alternatively how many pages a given text will make.

Cheshire labels Address labels which are printed on computer paper which can then be stuck on to envelopes by a special machine.

Collating A bindery operation putting sheets or more usually sections (printed and folded sheets) into the correct order.

Controlled circulation A magazine which is sent free of charge to the recipient and which relies for its income on advertising sales.

80 Publishing Your Own Specialist Magazine

Copy The (usually typewritten) words that have to be edited, marked up by the designer, and then typeset.

Creditors Suppliers to whom you or your company owe money. If you operate a subscription service it is worth noting that subscribers are also creditors to the value of the unexpired portion of their subscription.

Cutting out Making a particular image in a photograph or illustration stand out by cutting around the perimeter of the image shape and reproducing it without the background. These days more usually done by computer than a scalpel or brush.

Debtors People or companies who owe you money.

Dummy An example, sometimes very finished, sometimes not, of the finished magazine.

Em The square around a particular size of type: sometimes used to mean the 12 point or pica (the old name) unit of measurement which was the printers standard measure.

En Half an em.

EPOS Stands for 'electronic point of sale'. This is the system by which retailers can maintain accurate records of sales and stocks and for which bar codes are essential. It will not be very long before magazines which are not bar coded to fit in with retailers' EPOS systems will be totally excluded from sale in these outlets which will, of course, mean all the major chains.

Face The style or design of a particular type.

Fulfilment The process of sending out a mailing shot or a subscription run of a magazine.

Galley Continuous proofs of typesetting which are usually the first proofs to come from the typesetter.

Grid The basic skeleton of the page layout showing how many columns to the page, the type area etc.

GSM Grammes per square metre, the standard way in which paper weight is measured.

Gutter The inside margins of the page nearest the middle of the magazine. Pictures can (and frequently do) fall into the gutter.

IBC and **OBC** Commonly used abbreviations for 'inside back cover' and 'outside back cover' when referring to these spaces, usually for advertising purposes.

Glossary   81

Insert   A brochure or flyer inserted in the magazine. It can be either loose or bound into the publication.

Leading   (Pronounced as in wedding). The space between lines of typesetting.

List broker   An individual or company whose business is selling or renting lists which he owns or has an agency for.

Literals   Spelling and punctuation errors.

Mark-up   This is the specification of all the details to do with setting the copy. The mark-up is the copy with instructions to the typesetter written on it.

Mast-head   The main banner headline at the top of a page, usually used in connection with the title of the publication on the cover.

Measure   The width of a line of typesetting.

Media pack   The information sent to a prospective advertiser by a magazine. It might consist of a rate card, a recent copy or copies of the magazine, circulation breakdown and readership survey, sales by region or country, future editorial features and so on.

OCR system   Stands for 'optical character recognition', a fast developing piece of print technology which enables typescript to be read by computer and put on to disk for typesetting.

One shot   A one-off publication, usually arising from an existing magazine, which is published to cover a particular event or subject. These tend to have a longer life on the news stand than an issue of a magazine but are often unpopular with distributors.

Origination   A word usually used to describe the process of taking artwork to film.

Ozalid   Sometimes called a 'blue' (although they can be brown!) they are final proofs for last-minute checking before the magazine goes to press.

Paste-up   Paradoxically pasting down corrected typesetting, borders and so on, to produce final artwork for camera.

Perfect binding   Used for magazines with a high page content, usually over 64 pages, where the pages are glued to the cover, giving the publication a square back.

82 Publishing Your Own Specialist Magazine

Pica See em and en.

Plates Sheets of metal of a fairly thin gauge which in offset lithography have the printing image etched into them before they are wrapped around the printing press rollers.

Point A typesetting measurement for sizes of type. This sentence is set in 10pt type.

Prelims The preliminary pages of a publication, which usually contain the contents.

Progressives In colour printing these are proofs of each of the four colours and their combinations produced from the separations which are used as a guide for final printing.

Proofreading Checking the proofs supplied by typesetter or printer for accuracy.

Rate card A document issued by the publisher to prospective advertisers setting out the advertising rates, mechanical details and terms and conditions.

Readership Readership and sales are not necessarily the same thing. Surveys show that most magazines have a higher readership than their sales. This is because people who have not bought it read the magazine; they have it given to them by a friend, find it in the dentist's waiting room, etc.

Repro After type has been corrected and proofed, 'repro' is supplied; it is a perfect proof on high quality paper ready for camera.

Rollout After a test mailing has been done on a particular list and proved to be successful, the use of the entire list is known as a rollout.

Roughs Design term for roughly prepared layouts showing how the final design might look. Finished roughs (better than rough roughs) are sometimes called for when a presentation is needed. Also called 'scamps', and little ones are 'thumbnails'.

Saddle stitch A common method of binding using wire staples in the back or 'spine' of a magazine.

Sale or return A common method of supply to magazine distributors in which copies are supplied to the distributor who pays only for those copies sold. The unsold magazines are rarely returned.

Glossary 83

Screen Half tones have to be screened (the image broken up into dots) before they can be printed. Screen densities vary according to the subject and the kind of paper to be printed on.

Separations Sheets of film which are produced from artwork and transparencies and from which printing plates are made.

Series discount The discount which is given to advertisers for a sequential booking of advertising spaces, usually over 3, 6 or 12 issues.

Serif There are two different sorts of typeface, serif and sanserif. Serif typefaces have short lines at right angles to the main strokes of the letter, usually at the bottom, like feet, and sometimes at the top of the stroke. Sanserif type hasn't. This text is set in serif type; Figure 5.3 on page 57 is in sanserif.

Single-column centimetre (SCC) The usual unit of advertising space measurement.

Special position These are advertisement positions requested by advertisers which are not normally on offer, or have been selected by the magazine as being better spots than others for some reason, and they will usually cost more as a result.

Spread Printed matter or illustrations spread across adjacent columns or a double page opening in a book or magazine; (DPS = double page spread).

Sub-editing Preparing the text ready for the printer by ensuring consistency, correct spelling and grammar and inserting headings etc as necessary.

Teaser lines Sometimes called 'straplines' or 'coverlines', these are the lines of type on the cover used to describe articles inside the magazine.

Trade magazine A term used to denote a magazine which exists to serve a particular business or industry.

Typeface A particular kind of type design, of which there are many. Commonly used typefaces are Times and Helvetica.

Wordage Number of words in a piece of text.

Useful Addresses

Trade organisations

These listings do not claim to be comprehensive, but are merely intended as a guide.

The Association of Mail Order Publishers
1 New Burlington Street
London W1X 1FD
071-437 0706

Association of Subscription Agents
Periodicals Division
PO Box 410
Beaver House
Hythe Bridge Street
Oxford OX1 2SN
0865 792792 ext 212

Audit Bureau of Circulations (ABC)
13 Wimpole Street
London W1M 7AB
071-631 1343

British Amateur Press Association
73 Wickham Avenue
Bexhill
East Sussex TN39 3ES

British Printing Industries Federation
11 Bedford Row
London WC1R 4DX
071-242 6904

Chartered Society of Designers
29 Bedford Square
London WC1B 3EG
071-631 1510

Institute of Trade Mark Agents
4th Floor
Canterbury House
2-6 Sydenham Road
Croydon
Surrey CR0 9XE
081-686 2052

Periodical Publishers Association
Imperial House
15-19 Kingsway
London WC2B 6UN
071-379 6268

National magazine distributors

AGB Impress
Cloister Court
22–26 Farringdon Lane
London EC1R 3AU
071-253 3456

Comag
Tavistock Road
West Drayton
Middlesex UB7 7QE
0985 444055

IPC Magazines
Kings Reach Tower
Stamford Street
London SE1 9LS
071-261 5000

*Quadrant Publishing
Services*
Quadrant House
The Quadrant
Sutton
Surrey SM2 5AS
081-643 6800

SM Magazine Distribution
6 Leigham Court Road
London SW16 2PG
081-677 8111

UK Serials Group
114 Woodstock Road
Witney
Oxon
0993 703 466

Overseas distributors

A Cricus
*Agence & Messageries de la
Presse SA*
Rue de la Petite Ile 1
B-1070 Bruxelles
Belgium

H D Schrijver
Betapress BV
PO Box 77
Burg-Krollan 14
NL 5126 ZH Gilze

Steven S Brooks
*Dansk Bladdistribution
Aktieselskab*
PO Box 1918
Ved Amagerbanen 9
DK-2300 Copenhagen S
Denmark

Barrie Hitchon
Gordon & Gotch (NZ) Ltd
POB 3207
Auckland
New Zealand

Michael Jacovides
*Hellenic Distribution Agency
(Cyprus) Ltd*
POB 4508
2E Chr Sozou Street
Nicosia
Cyprus

Christopher A Hadzopoulos
Hellenic Distribution Agency
1 Digeni Street
GR-174 56 Alimos
POB 3315
GR-102 10 Athens
Greece

Useful Addresses 87

Massimo R Tarocco
Intercontinental SRL
Via Veracini 9
I-20124 Milano
Italy

Egon Moret
Kiosk AG/SA Le Kiosque
Maulbeerstrasse 11
CH-3011 Bern
Postfach 2668
CH 30011 Bern
Switzerland

Paul Faber
Messageries Paul Kraus
11 Rue Christophe Plantin
L-2339 Luxembourg

Gerhard Loidl
Morawa & Co
PB 159
Wollzeile 11
A-1011 Wien
Austria

Michael Sommer
Naville SA
Rue Levrier 5–7
CH-1201 Geneve
Switzerland

Joel Fillon
*Nouvelles Messageries de la
Presse Parisienne NMPP*
BP 13602
111 Rue Réaumur
F-75060 Paris-Cedex 02
France

Rose-Marie Lindh-Vos
Plus Grossist AB Interpress
Strandbergsgatan 61
S-11289 Stockholm
Sweden

Raimo Hertto
Rautakirja Oy
Koivuvaarankuja 2
SF-01640 Vantaa 64
Finland

Rolf Langlotz
W E Saarbach GmbH
PO Box 1562
Hans-Bockler Strasse 19
D-5030 Hurth-Hermulheim
Federal Republic of Germany

Rene Studer
Schmidt-Agence AG
Sevogelstrasse 34
CH-4052 Basel
Switzerland

Frank Martin
*Sociedad General Española
de Libreria (SGEL)*
Av Valdelaparra-39
E-28100 Alcobendas (Madrid)
Spain

Eri M Steimatzky
Steimatzky Ltd
Steimatzky House
11 Hakishon Street
PO Box 1444
Bnei Brak 51114
Israel

Subscription handling and mailing distribution companies

Advertising Services
Unit 1
Ely Road Industrial Units
Sutton
Ely
Cambridge CB6 2QD
0353 778905

Askew Mailing Services
1 Broadmead Business Park
Broadmead Road
Stewartby
Bedford MK43 9NX
0234 766819

Baileys Subscription Services
Warner House
Folkestone
Kent CT19 6PH

Mailbird Ltd
11 Roslin Square
Roslin Road
London W3 8DH
081-993 6116

Quadrant Subscription Services
Oakfield House
Perrymount Road
Hayward Heath
West Sussex RH16 3DH
0444 440421

Select Subscriptions
5 Riverpark Estate
Billett Lane
Berkhamsted
Hertfordshire HP4 1HL
0442 876661

Stonehart Subscription Services
Unit 1
Hainault Road
Little Heath
Romford
Essex RM6 5NP
081-597 7335

Subscription agencies

Bumpus, Haldane & Maxwell
Journals Subscription
Division
Cowper Works
Olney
Buckinghamshire MK46 4BN

W D Dawson & Son
Cannon House
Folkestone
Kent CT19 5EE

Delsa Import de Publicaciones
Serrano 80
Madrid 6
Spain

Esselte Tidskriftscentralen
Subscription Services
Box 45150
S-104 Stockholm
Sweden

International Subscription Agencies Pty Ltd
PO Box 709
Toowong
Queensland 4066
Australia

Jul & Gjellerup Books Ltd
31–33 Fiolstraede
DK-1171 Copenhagen K
Denmark

Librairie Payot SA
Rue de Bourg 1
1003 Lausanne
Switzerland

Martinus Nijhoff Subs Agents
PO Box 269
2501 AX The Hague
Netherlands

Maruzen Company Ltd
Journal Division
3-10 Nihonbashi 2-Chome
Chuo-Ku
Tokyo 103
Japan

Munksgaard
35 Norre Sogade
DK-1370 Copenhagen K
Denmark

Read More Publications Inc
140 Cedar Street
New York
NY 10006
USA

W H Smith & Son Ltd
Greenbridge Road
Swindon SN3 3LD
0793 616161

Stern-Verlag Jansse & Co
Friedrichstrasse 25–26
PO Box 7820
4000 Dusseldorf
Federal Republic of Germany

Swets Subscription Service
PO Box 830
2160 SZ Lisse
Netherlands

Consolidators and shippers

Groupex Transport International
Units A1 and A2
Star Business Centre
Marsh Way
Rainham
Essex RM1 38UH
04027 25544

Livingstone International Freight
Livingstone House
International Avenue
Heston
Hounslow
Middlesex
081-759 4771

90 **Publishing Your Own Specialist Magazine**

Mercury SDS
Unitair Centre
Great South West Road
Feltham
Middlesex TW14 8NJ
081-890 9833

Pharos Distribution Services
5-11 Lavington Street
London SE1 0NZ
071-261 9704

Computer companies specialising in publishing

The Computer Centre
Computer House
26 Gloucester Place
Brighton BN1 4AA
0273 693477

Graham Jones Consultancy
PO Box 43
Newbury
Berkshire RG13 4WH
0635 71803

Data Revue
Sutton Place
49 Stoney Street
Nottingham NG1 1LX
0602 58702

The Media Services Group
20-26 Brunswick Place
London N1 6D2
071-490 1830

Electronic Publishing
7-15 St Johns Terrace
Northampton NN1 1HA
0604 33464

*Woodall Publishing Services
Ltd*
260 Pentonville Road
London N1 9JY
071-278 2607

Typesetters

Express Typesetters
11 Riverside Park
Dogflud Way
Farnham
Surrey GU9 7UG
0252 724112

York House Ltd
York Avenue
Hanwell
London W7 3HY
081-840 1063

Lithoimage
Unit 4
Eagle Close
Arnold
Nottinghamshire
0602 670455

Sheet-fed printers

A selection of printers from various parts of the UK who specialise in magazines and periodicals.

Balding and Mansell Plc
Park Works
103 Norwich Road
Wisbech
Cambridgeshire PE13 2AX
0945 582011

Burgess and Son (Abingdon) Ltd
Thames View
Abingdon
Oxfordshire OX14 3LE
0235 555555

Ditchling Press Ltd
Consort Way
Burgess Hill
West Sussex RH15 9JT
0444 243253

Garnett Dickinson Print
Eastwood Works
Fitzwilliam Road
Rotherham
Yorkshire S65 1JU
0709 364721

Grange Press
Butts Road
Southwick
Shorcham
East Sussex BN4 4EJ
0273 592244

Magazine Printing Company
25 Mollinson Avenue
Brimsdown
Enfield EN3 7NT
081-805 5000

Mainsprint
Cadszow Industrial Estate
Hamilton
Strathclyde ML3 7QU
0698 282714

Presscraft
Unit 111
Hartlebury Trading Estate
Nr Kidderminster
Worcestershire DY10 4JB
0299 251360

Riverside Press
Thanet Way
Whitstable
Kent CT5 3JQ
0227 261364

Robert Stace and Co
Chalklin Works
Longfield Road
Tunbridge Wells
Kent TN2 3ET
0892 24225

Staples Printers
Trafalgar Road
Kettering
Northamptonshire NN16 8HA
0536 83401

Surrey Fine Art Press
Cavendish Road
Redhill
Surrey RH1 4AH
0737 761143

92   **Publishing Your Own Specialist Magazine**

Westdale Press
Unit 70
Portmanoor Road Industrial
Estate
East Moors
Cardiff
Glamorgan CF2 2MB
0222 461363

Web-offset printers

Chase Web St Austell
PO Box 3,
St Austell
Cornwall PL25 3JL
0726 66441

Cooper Clegg
Shannon Way
Tewkesbury Industrial Estate
Tewkesbury
Gloucestershire GL20 8HB
0684 850050

E T Heron
Silver End
Witham
Essex CM8 3QD
0376 83275

Hunterprint Group
Saxon Way East
Oakley Hay Industrial Park
Corby
Northamptonshire NN18 9EX
0536 747474

Kingfisher Web
Storey Bar Road
Eastern Industry
Peterborough PE1 5YS
0733 555567

Passmore International
Tovil
Maidstone
Kent ME15 6XA
0622 59931

Thomas Reed Printers
Double Century House
High Street West
Sunderland
Tyne and Wear SR1 1UQ

Yorkshire Web Offset
47 Church Street
Barnsley
Yorkshire S70 2AS
0226 734734

Colour origination and repro

Adroit Photo
Cecil Street
Birmingham B19 3ST
021-359 6831

Calligraphics
26 Queen Street
Oadby
Leicestershire LE2 4NJ
0533 720950

Useful Addresses 93

Colorworks
67-77 Chatsworth Road
Chesterfield
Derbyshire S40 1YB
0246 220333

D S Colour
2-18 Britannia Row
London N1 8HQ
071-359 8231

GKD Litho
Strawberry Street Industrial
Estate
Hull HU9 1EZ
0482 213287

Horizon Repro
27 Manasty Road
Orton Southgate
Peterborough PE2 0UP
0733 238400

Magnet Litho
Unit F
Tomo Estate
Packet Boat Lane
Cowley
Middlesex UB8 2JP
0895 440848

Optoscan
1 Hartlebury Mews
Hartlebury Trading Estate
Hartlebury
Nr Kidderminster
Worcestershire DY10 4JB
0299 251555

Saxon Photolitho
Saxon House
Hellesdon Park Road
Drayton High Road
Norwich NR6 5DR
0603 789560

Further Reading

Magazine Week (Wednesdays)

Chapter 1: **Financial Planning**
The Business Plan Workbook, Colin and Paul Barrow (Kogan Page) 1988
The Cash Collection Action Kit, Philip Gegan and Jane Harrison (Kogan Page) 1990
Debt Collection Made Easy, Peter Buckland (Kogan Page) 1987
Financial Management for the Small Business (2nd edition), Colin Barrow (Kogan Page) 1988

Chapter 2: **Marketing and PR**
The Business of Women's Magazines, Brian Braithwaite and Joan Barrell (Kogan Page) 1988
How to Market Books, Alison Baverstock (Kogan Page) 1990
How to Promote Your Own Business, J Dudley (Kogan Page) 1988
How to Write Articles for Profit and PR, Mel Lewis (Kogan Page) 1989
Practical Marketing, David H Bangs (Kogan Page) 1989
Sales Promotion, Julian Cummins (Kogan Page) 1989
Successful Marketing for the Small Business (2nd edn), Dave Patten (Kogan Page) 1989

Chapter 3: **The Role of the Editor**
The Art of Picture Research, Hilary Evans (David and Charles) 1979
Copy Editing: The Cambridge Handbook (2nd edn), Judith Butcher (Cambridge University Press) 1981
Editing for Desk Top Publishing, John Taylor (Gordon Fraser) 1988
A Handbook of Copyright in British Publishing Practice (2nd edn), J M Cavendish (Cassell) 1984
Hart's Rules for Compositors and Readers at the University Press, Oxford (39th edn), (Oxford University Press) 1983
The Oxford Dictionary for Writers and Editors (Oxford University Press) 1981

96 **Publishing Your Own Specialist Magazine**

The Picture Researcher's Handbook (3rd edn), ed Hilary Evans (Van Nostrand Reinhold) 1986
Pictures on a Page, Harold Evans (Heinemann) 1978

Chapter 4: **Design**
Design for Desk Top Publishing: A Guide to Layout and Typography on the Personal Computer, John Miles (Gordon Fraser) 1987
A Manual of Typography, Ruari McLean (Thames and Hudson) 1980
Type and Colour: A Handbook of Typography in Graphic Design, Michael Beaumont (Phaidon) 1987

Chapter 5: **Production**
Introduction to Print Buying, Michael Barnard (Blueprint) 1988
Magazine and Journal Production, Michael Barnard (Blueprint) 1986

Chapter 6: **Advertising**
British Rate and Data (monthly) McLean Hunter

Index

Accountancy 16
Advertising 13, 61-8
  commission 14
  press 26
  production 67-8
  rates 61

Banks and accountants 16-18
Back numbers 77
Bad debts 19, 68
Banks 16, 18
Bar codes 76
Binding 56
British Rate and Data (BRAD)
  62
Brochures 23, 24-5
Bromides 52
Business plan 16

Camera ready copy 39
Cash flow 11, 15, 57
Casting off 52
Classified advertising 61, 62
Computer companies 91
Consolidators and shippers 89
Contributors 34
Controlled circulation 11
Copy 52
  dates 67
Costs 14-15
Covers 43, 46
CRC (camera ready copy) 39
Credit 59
Credit cards 23
Credit control 18
Creditors 15

Design 41-6
Desk-top publishing 53

Direct mail 22
Directory of British Associations
  23
Discounts 64, 69
Distribution 16, 69-77
Dummy 66, 74

Editing 30-40
  copy 38
  schedules 38
Electronic point of sale 76
EPOS 76
Estimate 58
Exchange & Mart 61
Expenses 34

Finance and planning 9-19
Finishing 56
Flat plans 36, 37
Format 31
Fulfilment house 77

Glossary 79-83
Gravure 47
Grids 46

House style 34-5

Inserts 64

Layout grids 44-5
Letterpress 47
Letter spacing 52
Libel 35
Local radio 29

MAGSTAR rail delivery 74
Mail order sales 23-5
Mailsort 72

98 Publishing Your Own Specialist Magazine

Marketing 20–27
Mast-head 43

National magazine distributors
    86
Newsagent sales 12, 13, 16, 73

OCR 53
Offset lithography 48
Optical character recognition 53
Order forms 24–5
Overdrafts 18
Overheads 11, 17
Overseas distribution 76
Overseas distributors 86
Overseas trade sales 13

Page plans 38–9
Paper 49–50
Perfect binding 56
PIMS Media Directory 27
Platemaking 54
Point of sale material 26
Press advertising 26
Press releases 28
Pricing 20, 21, 31
Printers 56, 91
Printing 47–9, 56–60
Product 20, 21
Production 47–60
    costs 14
Profit and loss 10, 11–16
Progressives (proofs) 54
Promotion 22
    brochure 24
    costs 15, 20, 22

Proof correction marks 32–3
Public relations 27–9, 40

Rate card 62–3
Revenue 13

Saddle stitching 56
Sale or return 73
Scanning 54
Schedules 38, 59
Screen 54
Space selling 65–7
Specialist trade sales 12–13
Specification 57
Subscriptions 11, 13, 21
    agencies 88–9
    handling and distribution
        companies 88
    income 15
    lists 70
    mailings 14, 15, 72
    renewal 71
    sales 69–73

Teaser lines 46
Trade organisations 85
TV 29
Typefaces 51
Typesetters 90
Typography 43

Unsolicited articles 35

Web offset 48
Wholesalers 75